Dear Lucy

Thank you
all of your fri...
partnership, and sup!
through all the years
we worked together to
make waves!

♡ CH

Praise for *Making Waves*

"What glass ceiling? Lisa Lutoff-Perlo has disrupted an international industry with her vision and ability to break down barriers in pursuit of inclusion and humanity. The way she moves through the world with this singular focus is inspirational and precisely the example of the leadership necessary in any business. Frankly, I'm in awe of her."

—Nate Berkus, American Interior Designer, TV Personality

"When you think about navigating success, you go to the master of the industry and there is no one quite like Lisa Lutoff-Perlo. Her strength is taking leadership well beyond the norm with a unique combination of wit, vulnerability, and compassion. She set a course for success from the moment she took command and continues to make waves by paying it forward with grace, empathy, determination, and a passion for people."

—Captain Kate McCue, Celebrity Cruises

"Lisa Lutoff-Perlo is exactly the person you want to follow. I personally witnessed Lisa during my time on board one of her ships and I could see she had her heart invested with her employees from the cleaners to the bridge team. Lisa worked her way up to become CEO and it's clear she was called to lead because of her actions, her heart, and her vision. I will now use her leadership tips on board the vessels I run. Thank you, Lisa, for parting the seas for women at the helm."

—Captain Sandy Yawn, World-Renowned Captain, Author, International Speaker, and Businesswoman

"Lisa Lutoff-Perlo is a trailblazer who has made extraordinary waves for women, myself included. She has shown us that transforming an industry and centering diversity, equity, and inclusion is not only possible but can be done with grace. Her story of bravery and resilience makes this a must-read."

—Reshma Saujani, Founder and CEO, Moms First and Founder, Girls Who Code

"When I first met Lisa, I remember walking away feeling energized and excited. But it wasn't just the design and the challenge; it was having a feeling in my stomach that this was a woman who would take risks, break the mold, and transform an industry. Lisa has the ability to allow you to use your creativity without boundaries and take risks, and that is rare today."

—Kelly Hoppen, CBE, Award-Winning International Designer

"In *Making Waves*, Lisa challenges conventional notions of leadership and guides her team to the edge, where trust and empathy are fundamental. By fostering an environment of open communication and psychological safety, she cultivates a stronger bond among team members. Lisa's transformative leadership inspires others to redefine their approach. This book is the new standard in leadership . . . another first among many for a once-in-a-generation leader."

—Anthony Melchiorri, President, Argeo Hospitality

"In *Making Waves*, Lisa Lutoff-Perlo shares exactly what it takes to crash glass, cement, and bamboo ceilings! This book is a powerful resource for women of all races, cultures, and backgrounds seeking development and improved performance, and ways they, too, can find their superpower and soar in their careers."

—Dr. Sheila Robinson, Publisher and CEO,
Diversity Woman Media

"With humor, self-awareness, authenticity, and amazing storytelling, Lisa charts a path for all of us to become the leaders we are capable of becoming."

—Cindy Solomon, CEO, The Courageous Leadership Institute

"Lisa Lutoff-Perlo has legendary status in the travel industry for forging a path for women into senior roles in a traditionally male-dominated industry. A trailblazing, determined, and visionary leader, Lutoff-Perlo's story will inspire and empower other women to follow their dreams, never losing their authenticity or compassion for others. She writes with honesty, integrity, warmth, and passion about her career, her values, and the obstacles she faced on her journey to the top. Every young woman with aspirations should read this book."

—Lucy Huxley, Editor-in-Chief, *Travel Weekly UK*

"Lisa Lutoff-Perlo is not only inspirational but aspirational, both as a person and a leader. From her humble beginnings growing up playing in the seas of Boston to navigating previously uncharted waters in so many ways, Lisa is the example of hard work, determination, family-first mentality, and vision coming to fruition. CEOs change their organizations, often in reaction to daily events. As CEO of Celebrity, Lisa not only changed today but tomorrow and beyond."
—Dr. Jacqueline A. Travisano, Executive Vice President and Chief Financial Officer, Wake Forest University

"Lisa Lutoff-Perlo is one of the most transformative leaders of the 21st century, and this book serves as a beacon of inspiration and a testament to the indomitable human spirit. *Making Waves* encapsulates the essence of courage, transformation, innovation, and the steadfast belief in creating opportunities for those who deserve them."
—John Wensveen, Chief Innovation Officer, Nova Southeastern University and Executive Director, Alan B. Levan | NSU Broward Center of Innovation

"Lisa has extraordinary vision to see what others don't. And what makes that gift even more magical is how she understands the power and the importance of culture to lead and inspire an entire organization toward achieving what many can't even dream."
—Susan Bonner, Chief Commercial Officer, OneSpaWorld

"*Making Waves* is a must-read for anyone that aspires for leadership, especially women. Lisa Lutoff-Perlo shares heartfelt personal stories, hard-earned lessons learned, and extraordinary perseverance on every page. She combines an expansive vision, a keen sense of how to delight customers, and an eagerness to roll up her sleeves to get things done as a team. It's no surprise that Lisa is beloved for her all too rare, yet much needed, ability to take care *and* take charge. She is a role model of walking the talk as seen in her advocacy of women and underrepresented people. She does it all with authentic confidence, humility, and humor. Highly recommend!"
—Ellen Connelly Taaffe, Author, *The Mirrored Door*; Director, Women's Leadership Program and Clinical Associate Professor, Kellogg School of Management; Board Director, AARP Services, Inc.; and former Fortune 500 Executive

"The trajectory of Lisa Lutoff-Perlo's career represents an uncommonly rapid ascension—marked by industry revolution and transformational success. Her consistency in exceeding performance measures while maintaining winning cultures is attributable to her steadfast commitment to, and investment in, best-in-class strategic planning, cross-functional professional development, and authentic leadership. *Making Waves* tells the story of what it takes to be the best—and how to do it the right way—while capturing the contagious spirit of one of the most dynamic and influential leaders of our time."

—Dr. Jason Wingard, former President,
Temple University; Executive Chairman, The Education
Board, Inc.; and Author, *The College Devaluation Crisis*

"I've always believed human connection is a key responsibility of leaders, especially in an era where too often our attention is monopolized and monetized through fear and divisiveness. Lisa has exercised the kind of open-hearted leadership that not only positively affected all those whose lives have been enriched by her, but that serves as a model for future leaders. Dr. Bréne Brown says, 'Dare to lead,' and we're all the more grateful that Lisa did."

—Matthew D. Upchurch, CTC and CEO, Virtuoso

"*Making Waves* is a powerful story of courage and perseverance. Lutoff-Perlo's experiences and wisdom shared in this book will empower women and men to navigate their own paths to success while staying true to themselves."

—Can Faik, Award-Winning Journalist and
Cofounder, Global Hospitality Talk

MAKING WAVES

MAKING WAVES

A Woman's Rise to the Top Using Smarts, Heart, and Courage

Lisa Lutoff-Perlo

with Sarah McArthur

Matt Holt Books
An Imprint of BenBella Books, Inc.
Dallas, TX

Matt Holt is an imprint of BenBella Books, Inc.
10440 N. Central Expressway
Suite 800
Dallas, TX 75231
benbellabooks.com
Send feedback to feedback@benbellabooks.com

BenBella and *Matt Holt* are federally registered trademarks.

Printed in the United States of America
10 9 8 7 6 5 4 3 2 1

Library of Congress Control Number: 2023033575
ISBN 9781637744802 (hardcover)
ISBN 9781637744819 (electronic)

Editing by Lydia Choi
Copyediting by Scott Calamar
Proofreading by Christine Florie and Cape Cod Compositors, Inc.
Text design and composition by PerfecType, Nashville, TN
Cover design by Brigid Pearson
Cover photo © Michel Verdure
Printed by Lake Book Manufacturing

Special discounts for bulk sales are available. Please contact bulkorders@benbellabooks.com.

To Sophia and Jillian
You are my hope and inspiration

CONTENTS

FOREWORD

Bob Sullivan

As a media executive in the travel industry for several decades, I've had a privileged perch from which to observe its development and meet the people who have shaped the way that consumers enjoy vacations. But in addition to the travel news—new leisure products, innovations, and trends—I've watched how the industry has also reflected society writ large, whether its changes in how upcoming generations travel differently from their parents or how companies within the industry have reacted to calls for more diversity and inclusion.

And part of what I love about my job is getting to know great leaders like Lisa Lutoff-Perlo.

I've had a front row seat to Lisa's career. When I was introduced to her three decades ago, she was a sales manager at Royal Caribbean International, and I was immediately struck by her boundless energy, quick wit, and pursuit of excellence—but perhaps most of all by the way she interacted with everyone she encountered, whether it was an executive higher up the chain or staff that she managed. She connected with everyone. I thought at the time that she clearly had the makings of a great leader.

The industry is filled with tremendously talented leaders. And it's very fulfilling to see when talent is recognized and someone like Lisa rises to great success. She has earned it every step of the way with a unique combination of strengths: determination, intellectual curiosity, and, importantly, a commitment to support everyone on her team. Her pursuit of excellence, her courage to tackle challenges, and her resolve to make difficult decisions has made her a core architect of the industry.

Importantly, she has used her position to challenge the status quo, from ship design to gender inequality and lack of diversity and inclusion.

While her impact on the industry is undeniable, she continues to blossom as her career moves from strength to strength. The traits that are the foundation of her success continue to grow, and her imprint on the cruise industry will continue to deepen. I have no doubt her legacy will continue to reverberate long after her career is over—she has truly helped make the travel industry a better place for everyone.

Today, I'm honored to call Lisa a friend, and I'm so glad to have the opportunity to put my observations of her career in print. When I was thinking about how to describe Lisa, I came up with the following list of adjectives: dynamic, courageous, fearless, soulful, impactful, authentic, passionate, innovative, collaborative, creative, elegant, purposeful, intentional, agile, resolved, persistent, driven, clear, adaptable, resilient, inclusive, kind, risk-taking, sincere, genuine, relentless, stylish, tireless, committed, and unique. She is tireless in striving to help humanity as she continues to raise the bar and make those around her better with her infectious spirit.

And how fortunate we all are that she has written a book laying out her approach.

As you read it, you're going to see a lot of what I saw when I met Lisa in person: courage, vision, transparency, and heart. She is the type of leader who listens carefully and, without ego, has the analytical skills to dissect issues, challenges, and opportunities and to come out on the other side with the best decision to move forward.

Her candor inspires everyone around her, and she inspires everyone she connects with to do their best, if for no other reason than they don't want to let her down. And she doesn't want to let you down, either. As a visionary, she could just require others to simply follow, but with Lisa, it's a two-way street: she's going to do everything she can to help everyone around her achieve success.

Even during the difficult pandemic years, when the US cruise industry was completely shut down, Lisa delivered a groundbreaking new family of ships. And when, with the death of her sister, tragedy struck her personally, she showed remarkable courage.

Lisa is a truly great leader. And in this no-holds-barred book, she presents ways we can all become better leaders.

The industry is coming out of its most challenging era. The stakes have never been higher to get the recovery right. Knowing Lisa as a leader and a person, I know she will bring her team, and the industry, to a better place.

So, get ready to enjoy an incredible book on leadership by a truly great leader. She is a powerful person we will not only want to read about but also to emulate.

Robert G. Sullivan
Chief Commercial Officer/President
Northstar Travel Group

OPENING

A Letter from Lisa

Dear Sophia & Jillian,

I'd never considered writing a book. It was the furthest thing from my mind. I never thought I had an interesting enough story to tell or that anyone would want to read it.

As the first woman president and CEO of a brand in our company and one of the very first in our industry, I've had the chance to speak to many girls, young women, women, and men about my journey. I have also had many conversations with professional women who have asked me how I navigated my career and to tell them about the lessons I learned along the way.

And the response I got from so many of those conversations was, "You need to write a book!" After I heard that so many times, I decided maybe I should think about it.

A big part of my motivation was the two of you. I think you know how important and special you are to Auntie. You are now grown women charting your own course and your own future, and I watch you every day with such pride and optimism for all that you will do and become. I will never forget the text your mom sent to me one morning with a quote she had just seen: "Teach your daughters more about shattering the glass ceiling and less about fitting into the glass slipper." She then said, "Thanks to you, my girls know all about shattering the glass ceiling." It touched me deeply. And I have never forgotten it. It's one of the main reasons I ended up, once again in my career, in this place where I never thought I would be: writing a book.

Making Waves is not just about my journey. Sure, it's been a wonderful and rewarding journey that I share throughout the book. It's also been a long and winding road—not without its challenges along the way—but I wouldn't trade it for anything. I started at the bottom and, after thirty years, I finally made it to the top. I worked hard and smart. I paid my dues and earned every promotion and opportunity I got along the way. *Making Waves* is all about the lessons I've learned on this incredible journey that's helped me become successful (when the odds might have been against me), a better leader, and a better person.

It's about taking chances. Taking risks. Not knowing where those chances and risks might take you but learning to embrace them and enjoy the ride. It's about never giving up despite the roadblocks you might run into time and time again. It's about being great at what you do but realizing you can't do anything alone and without help. And it's about showing vulnerability and proving skeptics wrong as you encounter them along the way.

It's about being in the moment and enjoying and embracing what's in front of you. And it's about doing it with passion, integrity, and positivity—even when that is really difficult.

My hope is that you, and all of the readers, will not only learn a bit more about me and my almost forty-year career but also be inspired by some of the lessons I've learned and find them useful as you navigate your own beautiful journeys. I love you both. Deeply.

Love, Auntie

MAKING WAVES

1

Sailing Through the Storm

"Never let a good crisis go to waste."

Winston Churchill

I t was March 8, 2020, the high point of my career and my tenure as president and CEO of Celebrity Cruises. *Celebrity Edge*, the first of five ships in our Edge Series, was launched to critical acclaim in late 2018, and Celebrity had just come off its most successful year in its history. We had won numerous industry and consumer awards and had the best financial performance in the history of the brand. Our guests and employees were happier than they had ever been with historic satisfaction and engagement scores, we were getting ready to take delivery of *Celebrity Apex* in just a few weeks, and I was embarking on the *Celebrity Edge* to sail on our history-making and barrier-breaking International Women's Day cruise.

There I was on the bridge of *Celebrity Edge*. On the surface, it looked like any other day at the navigational hub of the ship. Officers prepared to depart from port. The captain presided over maneuvering the bow thrusters and Azipods that manipulate its movements. Deck officers kept eagle eyes on the forward, aft, port, and starboard parts of the ship, watching as the moorings were released, keeping in close contact with other officers located throughout the ship. Everyone had a job. All were focused. All worked as a team with amazing precision, each officer knowing the responsibilities required of him. Or, in this historic case, her.

This was the culmination of many years of working with my amazing male colleagues and focusing with purpose and intention on balancing the gender makeup of our marine teams on board our ships.

So there we were with Captain Kate McCue, the first (and still only) American woman to helm a mega cruise ship, whose dreams of a career at sea started at the age of twelve and whose first maritime assignment was a stint working a Chiquita Brands International cargo ship, transporting bananas from Ecuador to California. There was the chief security officer, Mor "Mia" Segev, who also serves with the Israel Defense Forces' active reserve. Staff Captain Maria Gotor was a practicing attorney in Spain for many years prior to following her passion for being at sea. All told, our bridge crew of twenty-seven women represented sixteen different countries, including Finland, England, Bulgaria, and the Philippines. I watched them all with great pride and admiration.

A couple of days after the ship departed from port, I made my way into the Grand Plaza, the center and heartbeat of the ship, where 1,500 guests were gathering to celebrate. Milana Dortangs, our associate hotel director, was playing Van Halen on a purple electric guitar, the color of International Women's Day—today, I have that guitar hanging in my office. Captain Kate, the master of the vessel, was mixing and pouring martinis.

These women are not typical, stodgy leaders. They are talented, accomplished professionals who not only take their jobs seriously but also readily and joyfully show their humanity and have fun with our guests and their crew. And they in no way believe that minimizes the importance of who they are or what they do. Now that's just cool.

And the vibe was electric because our guests—some of whom had booked the cruise because of our celebration of International Women's Day, and others who'd had no idea— were responding with joy. The ship was vibrating with great energy. In that moment, it occurred to me that we'd made more progress than even I'd realized along every dimension of our brand. I just stood there and soaked it all in.

It was a special moment among many in my career that I will never forget. I will always remember the sense of pride I felt at that time. I was leading an amazingly successful brand and was part of creating a diverse and wonderful culture that our guests and crew members were also excited and proud to be a part of.

I remember thinking that, if I were to walk away the next day, this moment could be the mic drop. I was on a real high and riding a wave of joy—and I had no idea what kind of storm I would shortly head into.

A Rogue Wave Hits

In the weeks leading up to the day I embarked on *Celebrity Edge* for the International Women's Day cruise, COVID-19 was becoming more and more of a global concern, although no one truly understood the magnitude of it at the time. Three days into the cruise, I left the ship to go back to the office. In the short time I was aboard, the pandemic began ravaging the world, infecting people in a way so brutal that no one really knew what the extent of it was truly going to be.

I arrived back in Miami on a Wednesday night, went to the office on Thursday and Friday, and then went home for the weekend. On March 13, 2020, we announced our shutdown of US operations in line with the CDC order on the same day. On the next day, March 14, 2020, we announced a global suspension of our operations. Our company and the industry halted cruising.

By that point, we'd already been managing significant disruption due to COVID-19. Some ports, learning of infected guests aboard ships around the world, refused to allow those ships to dock. Cruises were canceled and itineraries were altered, beginning with Asia and expanding beyond. Guests and crew testing positive for the virus on board were quarantined.

The global suspension of cruise travel rapidly took the pandemic's impact on our industry to an even more complicated level. And that meant our work, the biggest challenge we've ever faced both as an industry and as individual brands, was only just beginning. As a result of the global suspension, my executive team at Celebrity and the entire executive team of the company pivoted from managing our day-to-day business and operations to focusing on getting ships into ports, debarking guests, and arranging flights to get them home safely.

The complexity only increased as countries and airlines shut down, refusing to allow their own citizens back to their homes. Ultimately, it took us until July to get our last guests home. During this same period, we were also navigating constantly changing regulations to repatriate twenty thousand crew members. It took us until August to get our last crew member home.

That first voluntary suspension lasted thirty days. All thirteen of our cruise ships, and over sixty of our company's ships, sailing itineraries in regions including the Galapagos, the Caribbean, South America, Asia, and Australia, immediately halted voyages. As a global company, we were navigating and negotiating with governmental regulations and different health authorities and protocols in more than sixty-five countries.

On top of this, two of our newest ships that were in various stages of construction at a shipyard in France were either ready to be delivered—and now had nowhere to go—or were facing construction delays, disruptions, and the implementation of many new protocols.

The pandemic not only required everything I knew and had accomplished to navigate my way through, but it also tested every leadership skill and value I had ever developed. But quitting was not an option. The words of legendary NFL quarterback Tom Brady (the GOAT) resonated with me every step of the way: "I didn't come this far to only come this far." I had to keep going.

While all of this was devastating, we still thought our operational pause would only last a couple of months and that we would be sailing again in June. Little did I know that it would be fifteen months before one of our ships would again sail out of a US port.

A Test Beyond All Tests

Focusing on these famous, inspiring words of Winston Churchill, keep going I did.

The shutdown was a profound test of my team's commitment, fortitude, and morale. There they were, working the hardest they'd ever worked, in uncharted territory within an industry that was simply closed for business. The day-to-day rewards of our jobs—seeing and hearing from happy guests, delivering award-winning vacations and experiences, and hosting memorable celebrations—had evaporated.

Small bubbles of optimism were continually burst by the sobering news of the day: the surges, the case counts, the latest rounds of closures and constraints, the canceled charters that were supposed to take our crew home, the continued shutdown of our industry months after we thought we would have been back sailing again.

And all through those months, our company teams were working around the clock chartering airplanes, working with governments and health agencies around the world, and finding access to tests and, ultimately, vaccines. It was a never-ending logistical nightmare. We all wondered if it would ever end.

This was all playing out against a backdrop of people across the world who were dealing with life-and-death issues. Our crew members and shoreside team members were likewise impacted by the loss of loved ones in those early weeks and months.

It wasn't until July of 2020 that all guests—and, early August, our final crew members, aside from the skeleton crew that would stay on board and keep ships functioning—were repatriated.

Once guests had all been debarked, it was time to focus on the mental and physical well-being of our crew members, many of whom would be staying aboard until their own governments would accept them back.

We had to follow draconian protocols; crew members were required to isolate from one another in staterooms by themselves. We moved them all to balcony staterooms so they could at least get fresh air outside. Meals were delivered and left by their doors. Our entertainment team put together shows for their fellow crew members virtually on Zoom. We created special menus featuring lobster and filet mignon, along with dishes based on the culinary traditions of crew members' countries. It was the least we could do to help get them through their days while we followed CDC requirements. It was heartbreaking for us and terribly difficult for them.

I felt such relief finally getting our crew home—and, later, the best part of returning to operations into service would be seeing them together again.

Digging Deep

As I look back at how I coped during this series of professional crises, there were also moments that reminded me how our world was moving forward in some ways. We took virtual delivery of *Celebrity Apex* two weeks after we shut down—another industry first—whose official launch and introduction would have to be postponed for some time (it remained at its French shipyard for months).

We were still building *Celebrity Beyond*, part of the Celebrity Edge Series, which gave us the opportunity to remain focused on our positive future and amazing new ships and brand. This is a lesson that I've realized is crucial when going through the most difficult of times: Find something positive for you and your team to focus on. We had something to look forward to. We were able to continue to be creative and innovative. We were focusing on the positive while the world and our industry were still accentuating the negative.

As I tried my best to be productive amid all the chaos, I learned yet another valuable lesson: I needed to compartmentalize each part of my life. I wish I could say the business part was the toughest one to get a handle on. But it wasn't.

The toughest part? My younger sister Dawn, whom I took care of from the time she was a baby, who lived with me for decades, and whom I adored (my sisters mean everything to me), was diagnosed with terminal cancer in April of 2020, one month after our shutdown. I wasn't sure how I was going to get through our business shutting down, let alone how I was going to cope with losing my sister, whom I had spent over sixty years taking care of and keeping safe.

> "This is a lesson that I've realized is crucial when going through the most difficult of times: Find something positive for you and your team to focus on."

On April 26, 2021, we did our virtual reveal (another industry and brand first) of *Celebrity Beyond*. I had a "starring" and live role in that reveal. This was a very important event for us. We needed to generate excitement and consumer demand and interest for this ship during the worst of times for our industry and our business. At the same time, my sister was losing her battle in another room in my home. But I had to be "on." I had to celebrate this amazing ship and all her wonder with consumer and trade press along with our trade partners. And, we had more people and press attending this virtual reveal than we would have had if we'd conducted it in person, so it was a big deal. We had so much riding on the success of this virtual launch.

I still don't know how I got through that moment. Somehow, I found the strength to just keep functioning, to do what I needed to do for the people I needed to do it for. **My lesson during this difficult time was that being a leader is not easy and takes strength you sometimes don't realize you have.** I knew I had to function at a high level. Too many people were depending on me for too much at that moment, and I couldn't let them down. So, I carried on and did what I had to do. And it was great.

Three days later, on April 29, 2021, we lost my sister. The worst day of my life.

In the days following the *Beyond* reveal, the headlines that were written about the ship were better than what we could have written ourselves. Our partnerships with Chef Daniel Boulud and Gwyneth Paltrow and Goop took center stage, and the ship was heralded as "luxury." Many noted that they didn't think the Edge Series could get any better, but *Beyond* was taking the series to the next level—"beyond" anything they could have imagined. Bookings came flooding in. By all measures, it was a resounding success.

Balance, What Balance?

At this point, I would like to talk about balance. And this is the only time I will talk about it. Countless times in interviews, women are asked how we balance our careers with our personal lives and responsibilities. This question never ceases to irritate me.

The lesson I have learned during all of my years of leadership is this: There is no balance. Our lives are constantly out of balance. We are reprioritizing constantly. And my belief is that as long as it all levels out at the end of the day, that's the best we can hope for. One hundred percent of my focus that day had to be on the *Celebrity Beyond* reveal, despite the unimaginable happening in my life.

Immediately after that reveal, I retreated. I spent the last days with my sister. I grieved. I gave myself and my family 100 percent. Because that's what I needed to do. Perfect imbalance. We have to stop apologizing and feeling guilty for that.

Throughout my almost forty-year career in the cruise industry, I never could have predicted the turmoil caused by the pandemic. It forced me to reevaluate the leadership qualities I had been developing for decades—namely, my determination, drive, and focus on achieving perfection and stellar results.

For the first six months of the crisis, I was consumed by the logistical and day-to-day challenges with getting our guests and crew members home safely. It was complicated. It was arduous. It wasn't just our industry closing down but also the whole world.

Focus on the Future

Months later, when the daily unknowns abated, I shifted my thinking toward how to use this pandemic as an opportunity to make our brand better and stronger. This pause in our business offered a chance to step back and reimagine our brand.

I wanted to find a way to inspire my team and all of the people working at Celebrity at the time. Each day was filled with unknowns. People were afraid our business and brand wouldn't survive. They feared for their livelihoods. I needed to do something, and fast. This was no way for any of us to feel every day until we got back into business, and I knew this was the perfect chance to implement change. I owed that to my team.

In the face of this unprecedented turmoil and crisis, I learned to dial up my inherent qualities, such as optimism, confidence, inspiration, vision, compassion, and communication, and let them take center stage and a more prominent role. And I also learned that other inherent qualities, like perfectionism, needed to take a back seat. For the time being, anyway. A valuable lesson in leadership: flex your style to fit the circumstances.

Maintaining a sense of optimism was truly a challenge for me, even though I am a pure and true optimist at heart. With what was going on in my personal life and my own concern about our business, I, too, had my doubts and fears. But I had to deal with those on my own time. I had to wake up every day and find the silver linings in the COVID-19 cloud. And there were many.

On the personal side, I was able to spend every day of the last year of my sister's life with her. That was a gift, one that we both treasured. That would never have happened had it not been for COVID-19. A silver lining.

I also needed to find a way to give myself and my team a sense of hope and purpose. What sustained me then, and now, is my belief in the trans-

> "A valuable lesson in leadership: flex your style to fit the circumstances."

formative power of travel and the enriching luxury of experiencing it on a cruise ship—and the knowledge that as human beings we cannot live or survive being shut off from each other and the world. By putting aside my own fears and focusing on all that I knew to be true, I learned that optimism becomes a self-fulfilling prophecy once you get others to believe that the future is bright and there is hope. As a leader, that's what people are counting on us for.

I've always operated looking forward to the future, never gazing too long into the rear-view mirror. My team will tell you one of my favorite phrases is "Don't let history dictate our future." That's just who I am.

Unfortunately, during the COVID-19 era, we needed to be in survival mode, and that meant the present took center stage.

I was asked every difficult question possible: How much equity do you have to raise to fulfill our burn rate and still have cash in the bank to make payroll? When are we going to get back into service? How many liquidity models and return-to-service plans are you building?

I was determined not to let these questions consume us. Instead, I wanted us to use this time to refine our strategy and continue to drive innovation for Celebrity. We brought in a luxury brand strategist to help us refine our positioning and experiences. And we made many changes as we figured out how we were going to come out of this pandemic, including our inclusive pricing strategy, our evolved experiences, a new brand moniker, and strengthened points of differentiation.

As a leader you have a choice—choose to channel yourself and your team with positive energy. While I watched leaders in our industry take a position of "Let's just ride out this storm until it's over," I chose differently. I wanted our team and our brand to come back stronger than ever, and I was not going to do what others were doing and wallow in the misery we had found ourselves in.

A commitment to innovation and making our comeback stronger than our setback became the rallying cry for our brand, allowing us to plan for the future rather than obsess over the uncertainty of a present that we had no control over. At this point, I saw a fundamental change in our people. They were hopeful. They were motivated. They were inspired. They believed in our future. And as a leader, there's not much more you can hope for, especially during the height of a pandemic when your business is completely shut down.

I remember being asked by one of the women coaches I had during this time, "Lisa, how is a person like you, who is always in control and feels like they can control every situation they are in, coping right now in an environment where you don't have any control?"

It was a thought-provoking question. But it was one that I realized I could answer because I had gained clarity about it during this terrible time—another silver lining in the COVID-19 cloud. I had learned that there are things I can control, and there are things I cannot control, and I'd decided to spend all of my time focusing on the former. My team and I worked on what we could control and let go of what we couldn't. Only then were we able to eventually come out on the other side in a productive way.

Leading from the Front

Another leadership attribute I needed to dial up during this time was communication. With our team and crew scattered around the globe as a general course of business, I've always made it my mission to communicate frequently, openly, and candidly. Everyone needs to see my face and hear my voice to believe my optimism is real and to get to know who I am.

I do not want to be an enigma. I want to be someone that our crew (from the front line to the captain) can relate to and someone they know who relates to them. That communication needs to occur regularly to maintain positive momentum and motivation—and to create confidence and optimism for a bright future. So, during our time out of service, I made it a point to communicate with our crew around the world through written and video messaging. It soon became clear that they believed we were going to come back, and they were eager to do so.

I've learned that leaders must lead with their hearts as well as their heads. During this time, I realized that I needed to dial up the heart because that's what my team, crew, guests, and stakeholders needed from me. Compassion. Empathy. Understanding. Hope.

They say a smooth sea never made a skilled sailor. The COVID rough seas we faced were, of course, unprecedented—our business and industry closed down for fifteen months. It was probably the worst storm I've had to face, and it won't be the last one I'll have to sail through. I think it's safe to say that all of us have had our fair share of rough seas in life. I know I have.

Ultimately, though, I know we come out of these storms stronger than before. Whether a business failure, a personally devastating experience, or a global pandemic, I've navigated through the storms of my life because I've learned that, by digging deep and finding my North Star, and by bringing things to the surface that have always been a part of my DNA, I can get myself and those around me through any challenge.

I had no idea when we would be back in business, especially as the months dragged on and we dealt with the CDC and health authorities around the world.

But I knew we would be back.

And I knew that when we did come back, I would want and need this same group of people with me. So, while others in our industry stalled and talked about doom and gloom every day, I did the opposite.

My methodology was hope and encouragement. My message was "We've got this." As a leader, I learned that I needed to be the difference maker my people needed me to be.

> **"As a leader, I learned that I needed to be the difference maker my people needed me to be."**

And it was all grounded in a firm belief in everything we had accomplished to get us to where we were before our world fell apart. I looked straight ahead, always recalling one of my favorite quotes: "Our future is not written yet. It's ours to write." And that's exactly what we did.

2

≈≈≈

Not Everyone Has a Plan

"It's not the destination, it's the journey."

**Ralph Waldo Emerson, American essayist,
lecturer, philosopher, abolitionist,
and poet, from "Self-Reliance"**

S ometimes the easiest way to begin is at the end, or at least at the present point, and then to work backward. Makes sense for someone who wasn't born with a plan for her life, doesn't it?

Some people know exactly what they want to do and accomplish and the steps they are going to take to get there. Many years ago, I was one of two women leaders speaking to an audience of young college women. The other speaker was a highly accomplished leader from a very prestigious company. We had been asked to speak to these young women getting ready to graduate about our lessons learned in leadership. As I listened to the other guest speaker, I was struck by how, at an early age, she'd known exactly what she wanted to do. She had been maniacally focused on her plan. She knew what she wanted, what she needed to do to get there, did those things, and then succeeded. She accomplished her goal, and she now had her dream job. And I remember thinking, "That's terrific. And that worked for her." That was how she'd come to be on that stage.

But I also couldn't help but notice how different our paths were. She'd known exactly what she wanted to achieve, planned for that outcome, and then tackled the steps to accomplish it. My journey was quite different. Totally the opposite. When I'm asked if I ever thought I was going to be president and CEO of Celebrity, I can answer definitively, "No. I never thought of myself in a role like this, and I did not have this in my plan."

As I got ready to speak, I was reminded that there is so much pressure on all of us, especially young people, to have a plan. Know what you want to study. Major in. Be. Accomplish. Can we all really do that? Is it fair to have such pressure when so much can change along the way? Is having a plan limiting? Does not having a plan mean you will never accomplish anything meaningful? I decided at that point I was going to tell my story, however unconventional, to this group of young women.

The first thing I said when I took the stage is that I really admire people who are so clear and determined, who know exactly what they want, and then take the steps they need to take to get it. And the second thing I said was: **"One of the lessons I learned on my journey was that not everyone has a plan. And that's okay."** The great news is that both the other leader and I ended up on that stage, so both approaches can work. They both can get you where you want to go or where you never, in your wildest dreams, thought you would end up. I wanted to reassure the young women in the audience that they can still succeed if they don't have a plan.

There's so much pressure when we're young: Will we have a career? Will we have a family? Can we have both? Where will we end up? Cut yourself some slack. If we give ourselves permission to be ourselves and embark on a journey that might not have a clearly defined destination, doing things because they make sense at the time and because they're aligned with who we are as people, we may not know exactly where we're going to end up, but chances are great that it's going to be even better than we could have planned.

A Leader from the Start

I grew up in Gloucester, Massachusetts. As the eldest of three sisters, I like to say I was born into a leadership position. From the time I was two, when our middle sister Dawn was born, I have been leading the way and caring for others. I believed from the moment she and then later my second sister, Bobbi, were born that I was supposed to take care of them and be the leader of our family. Our parents always worked at our coffee shop and then later at our restaurants, so we were latchkey kids from a very early age, and much of raising my sisters fell to me. I'd get them up in the mornings, make them brush their teeth, pack their lunches, and get them on the school bus. My teenage years were quite responsible while my friends were just having fun and being teenagers.

It could be tough and, sometimes, a little precarious. I didn't always know what I was doing. One night, I decided to make pork chops for dinner. Now, remember, I was pretty young, so I made them medium rare because I thought you cooked them just like you cooked steak. Our mom came home right about the time we were eating them, and she immediately called the doctor because we were eating "undercooked" pork. He said we would be okay. Whew! We survived. In thinking back on this and so many other memories from when we were growing up, I realize I have always run toward not just responsibility and caring for others but also into the unknown. It doesn't scare me; it's inherent in me. It is who I am, and I don't give it a second thought—unless of course, I'm writing a book about the lessons I've learned in leadership.

Like when I started first grade at St. Ann elementary school in Gloucester. I will never forget that first day of school. We were all standing in front of the school with our moms, and one of my classmates was crying inconsolably, absolutely terrified of walking into the classroom.

I instinctively walked over to her, took her by the hand, and told her it was going to be okay. She stopped crying, and we walked into our classroom together. I didn't think about what I did—it was instinct. It's still my instinct. I want everyone to come along, to be included, to be part of the adventure. To count on me to help ensure that everything will be okay. Isn't that what we need to do as leaders?

In high school, I could have been one of the popular girls, but instead I chose to hang out with the girls who weren't that popular, who weren't getting all the attention from the boys (ugh, high school). I shied away from the popularity contest because it was more important to me to be smart, get good grades, and befriend those who needed a friend. Being popular just wasn't important to me.

And this wasn't something I was taught. My mom is open and gregarious and makes the best of everything, but she never said, "Go take that little girl by the hand and help her overcome her fear" or "Go be friends with the unpopular girls—they need it a lot more than the popular ones."

The question that is often asked, "Are leaders born or made?" has long been the subject of debate. From my own experience, I'd say it's both. In thinking back on all of these experiences I have shared, I realize I have always been a leader. I believe leaders are born, and then we are shaped and fine-tuned by our experiences and life circumstances.

Making Change

My first job was at my parents' restaurant, the Harborview Coffee Shop, when I was six years old. For some crazy reason, I wanted to be put to work and kept asking for a job. Every morning, the milk company would deliver our milk in those little crates. When a crate was emptied, my mom would turn it over and stand me on it, and I would make change at the cash register for our customers who came in to buy their coffee to go. I loved working that register. It's been said that my first job was making change and that I'm still at it!

When I wasn't at school, I spent my time in our coffee shop and then, later, at our restaurants. Every weekend at five in the morning, our dad would get us up so we could get ready for work. We worked the breakfast shift. I spent every weekend working at the restaurant, serving and busing tables. I served the entire dining room by myself. It was a lot of work, but on the bright side, it taught me how to work a room and to not miss one person. **And I learned a valuable lesson: nothing happens for you if you aren't willing to put the work in.**

All of these experiences helped shape me as a leader. Through many decades, everything I do as a leader has been built on the essence of who I have been since a young child. Every day, I carry with me those early lessons I learned. There's just a lot more people and moving parts now.

I ended up in a place and position I never dreamed of. That's why I believe that if I can, anyone can. That might be an extreme statement, but it's true. If you have focus, drive, determination, and perseverance, anything is possible. It just takes dedication, time, consistency, and purpose. As I would tell my younger self: dream big.

The Floundering Years

I'm not an Ivy League graduate. I didn't start at the top or close to the top and then continue to rise. In fact, quite the opposite. On May 6, 1985, I began my career in our company going door-to-door to travel agencies convincing them to sell lots of our cruises to their customers. I still sometimes find it hard to believe that this "girl next door" who floundered in her twenties, seemingly without direction, went from entry-level sales to president and CEO of this multibillion-dollar brand in this great company.

Hospitality is what I know and do best, so I stayed in it. I had sales roles like selling conference and event space, and then my dad helped me get a position managing a nightclub in central Massachusetts. I was excited with this job, as it was the first one I had in management.

The thing was that it just wasn't me. Work started at 3 or 4 PM, and we closed around 2 AM. We would close the club and then go out to breakfast and not get home until 3 or 4 AM. And then do it all over again the next day.

I knew this wasn't where I wanted to be. The lesson I learned is that you might not know what you want or where you want to go, but you need to recognize what you don't want and where you don't want to be and make changes as needed.

So there I was one Sunday morning in 1983, lying in bed reading the help wanted section of the *Boston Globe*. I ran across an ad for a position selling group cruise travel for a big company called Crimson Travel. That sounded interesting. I'd never thought about doing that. What the heck? I decided I would give it a try. I had nothing to lose, and it would get me out of a situation I was unhappy in.

I interviewed and was hired to develop the cruise business for this agency that sold millions and millions of dollars of cruises.

While I was working at the agency, the sales rep for Royal Caribbean at the time came into the office and mentioned that he had just been promoted and was moving to Miami. He told us his job was open and that if we were interested, we should send our résumé.

I'd been at the agency for a year and the job wasn't really working out, so I said, "Why not? That sounds interesting. Working for a cruise line would be great and exciting." I ended up getting the job after fighting hard for it and not being hired the first time around. Another lesson I learned: never give up if you really want something.

I spent the next seventeen years in our sales organization. After four years in my first district sales manager role, I applied for and got a regional sales manager role and moved to South Florida. I started securing progressive and varied roles in the sales organization and loved it. I was prospering. I was rising within one company, whereas, prior to joining, I had switched jobs just about every year. And, wouldn't you know it—I finally realized, "I have a plan!" I wanted to be the head of sales. I worked hard toward that goal and was very successful in every position along the way. I excelled. And, eventually, I became the heir apparent to the sales head. I now knew what it felt like to have a plan, and I was really liking it.

And then my plan fell apart. The senior vice president of sales and marketing had a different plan for me. He decided I should gain new experience, and he was someone who believed that moving highly talented people into different roles in an organization was good for both the organization and for these workers' development. So, despite my protests, I was moved from sales to marketing. In my mind, my career and plan were over. So much for having a plan.

> **"I learned that when you take your circumstances and make the best of them, when you prove to people that you can pivot and learn and succeed despite the role you are in, this is what will serve you best."**

But I was not going to give anyone the satisfaction of thinking they'd derailed me. So, I made the best of it. I learned that when you take your circumstances and make the best of them, when you prove to people that you can pivot and learn and succeed despite the role you are in, this is what will serve you best. So that's what I did. And you know what? I really enjoyed the new role. I excelled in the areas I was responsible for, and I remember thinking, "I'm glad this happened. This is good for me."

And then my plan changed again. The same gentleman, who was also a big sponsor and advocate for me, decided it was time for me to move and change roles once more. "Okay," I thought. "What's next?"

In 2005, I moved to a new role in a new brand in a completely new discipline. It was as a vice president of onboard revenue, and I was very excited. That said, it was also a bit scary. I was a sales and marketing girl. What did I know about operations? I had been a part of one brand for twenty-one years, and now I was moving to a new one. I didn't know anything about this other brand or any of the people I would now be working with. But I put all of that aside and embraced the change, embraced the role.

I ended up learning so much about our business during the seven years I was in operations. I was promoted to senior vice president of hotel operations by the end of that time. I was able to have an impact on the culture, the growth of the brand, the new ships, the experiences for our guests, and the performance of the operation. I learned during those seven years that even though change like this can be a bit scary, without risk there is limited reward, and taking chances can often lead to much more and better opportunity. These new experiences were invaluable.

And then my boss, my sponsor, and my advocate left the company. Now what? More on some of this later, but within six months of his departure, I was moved again.

This next role was a promotion back to the original brand I had been with for twenty-one years, which was wonderful for my career trajectory. As the executive vice president of operations, I would not only be the head of hotel operations—I would also be responsible for marine operations. A first for me. A first for any woman in our company. A great opportunity. Another opportunity to learn and lead a new part of our business. And another opportunity to hone my leadership skills in unfamiliar territory. It was a great two years that I underestimated in terms of how it was going to help me build my career and achieve my ultimate goal. So I embraced the role, I accomplished many great things, and then, two years later, in December of 2014, I was finally appointed as president and CEO of Celebrity Cruises.

And that's how my story goes. It's an illogical and windy journey that has led me to where I am now. It wasn't easy every step of the way, and there were many forks in the road that didn't always make sense at the time. At one point in the journey, it became clear what I wanted and what I needed to do to achieve that goal, and I did eventually succeed in hitting that target—but, as Emerson says, it's not about the destination. It's about the journey—and the journey will certainly continue. That's how it's always been for me.

What I've learned is that not all paths are linear, and that a winding path allows you to gain experiences as a leader and professional that you never would have if you'd stayed on a linear road. I absolutely could have ended up being the head of sales. But then I never would have become the president and CEO of one of our brands. Every time I was given a new or different opportunity, I rose to the occasion. And that led me to be where I never thought I would end up.

If I'd had a plan earlier, would I have become president and CEO sooner? Perhaps, but I don't look at it that way. My career unfolded the way it was supposed to. I took risks. I went into positions that were not natural for me because I didn't have experience or subject matter expertise. I found a way to be successful even without that.

I want people to learn from what I've been able to accomplish without a plan and not be so hard on themselves to think they should have it all figured out. Number one, it puts a lot of pressure on you, and number two, it could ultimately be the thing that holds you back. I've learned that when you are agile, flexible, open, and willing to learn, it will lead you to your ultimate success.

Not having a plan has taken me on this incredible journey. The experiences I've had and the knowledge I've gained from them made me a very qualified candidate for the president and CEO role and made my transition into the role easier.

Because of my journey, I'm not a one-dimensional leader. While the foundation of who I am as a leader is the same wherever I lead, not having a plan has enabled me to build leadership strength in a holistic and comprehensive way.

No Matter What, Consistency Is Key

As I embarked on my career path, I had to learn many new areas of our company and brands. As I said earlier, I was not a subject matter expert in many of the new positions I was put into. Instead, I learned along the way thanks to the amazing people I have had the privilege to work alongside for well over three decades. I've learned you do not have to be a subject matter expert to try new things and go into areas or jobs that are exciting or appealing to you. There are other inherent leadership qualities that are more important than expertise.

Consistency is one of the qualities I've found critically important for leadership. I had the pleasure of working with a very smart young woman when I went into my first operational leadership role at Celebrity. She was such a help to me in assimilating into a new brand, role, and culture. We bonded quickly, as she was one of the leaders in the area that I was taking over. Within a short period of time, she moved into another area of responsibility as a high-potential talent that we were developing. After she left, she and I chatted about her new role and how she was doing. All was not going as well as she had hoped in her new area, and I remember her telling me that one of the things she really appreciated about working with me was that I was a leader who is consistent. She always knew where we were going, she told me. I always rallied a team around what we needed to do to get there, I stayed on course, and I didn't keep moving the goalpost. **I learned early on that it's not the task that is the most difficult for those who work for you: it's indecisiveness, changing direction, lack of clarity, and lack of vision that people find the most challenging in working for certain leaders. Don't be that leader.**

Moving the goalpost is very frustrating for people. They want to know where they are going and that everyone is headed in the same direction. Don't confuse people along the way; don't send some people one way and others a different way. If you keep shifting focus or direction, it will be difficult for people and limit their ability to be successful.

Consistency is probably one of the most important things about all of us. When we have it, others know what to expect—good or bad. People don't like dealing with a lot of surprises. Taking forks in the road and jumping around is disruptive, demotivating, and even demoralizing for people.

Consistency is more than the decisions we make—it is also about, maybe even more importantly, who you are as a leader.

Not All Paths Are Linear

I am fortunate to speak to many people on many occasions about their careers and their paths. Oftentimes, this happens within my own company. People want to understand how they can accomplish their own dreams and aspirations and would like to know the things I did that helped me accomplish mine. I am always flattered that others want to talk to me about that and always do my best to make time to share my story and whatever advice I can give them.

What I always find interesting as I am having these conversations is that, more often than not, the people I am talking to have a plan. They know what path they want to be on. That path is clear and, in most cases, completely linear. What I try to explain is that it's great they have a plan, but a plan can be limiting. Often, you need to move around to move up. And that doesn't have to stop you from getting to where you want to be.

> **"If you are not willing to learn, take a chance, or improve your knowledge, understanding, and value to yourself and your company, you are missing out on opportunities you don't even know exist."**

Most other executives I've worked alongside have, like me, had a varied and nonlinear career path to get to the wonderful positions they are in. Yet people continue to be reluctant to move out of their comfort zones or alter their original plans. I just don't understand it.

If you are not willing to learn, take a chance, or improve your knowledge, understanding, and value to yourself and your company, you are missing out on opportunities you don't even know exist that might come your way—opportunities that might take you somewhere great you never thought you'd get to.

3

Watch Me Prove You Wrong

**"Tell me I can't, then watch me work
twice as hard to prove you wrong."**

Heather Mitts, Olympic gold medalist

From No Plan to the Plan

My plan had been completely derailed when I was moved into a completely different role in a completely different place.

It was tough. I had to take that extreme disappointment, that frustration, and channel it into a positive direction. But perhaps my years of sales experience had prepared me for this disappointment and helped me to bounce back. In sales, that's what you do. You face rejection and get a lot of noes. You get knocked down, but you reboot and get back up and back at it. And perhaps it's just who I am. **I learned that it's important to turn the negatives into something positive.** And I relied on a lesson that I learned much earlier in my life: Never, ever, ever give up. Giving up is easy. Instead, you need to dig deep and put a plan together to prove that you will still be successful despite the hardship. You have to use positive energy to offset the negative things that will often come your way.

I've rebooted several times in my career. When I've been knocked down, I've gotten up absolutely determined to figure it out, to "prove them wrong," to succeed. A lot of people ask me how I've done it, but it's been at least slightly different every time.

I've learned to always focus on the attributes, skills, and talents that appear most helpful in a given situation, which might call for emotional intelligence, or courage, or optimism, or innovation, or boldness, or helping others do their jobs. Or all of them, or a combination of some of them. Whatever I do, though, I always focus on creating a positive outcome.

In times when I've been knocked down, I've also learned that I don't know everything—and that's okay. I've learned to find friends in the organization who can help, and I've learned to build my team so that they complement me in a way that'll help all of us be successful. I try to be very honest about identifying my gaps, which takes a lot of courage, and I have filled those gaps with those who have the experience and expertise that I do not. Self-awareness is critically important, but I have encountered and worked with so many who just don't have it.

Early in my career, this was hard for me—to admit that I didn't know everything. And I know it's hard for many others, too. I've seen many high-level leaders enter or advance in our organization and behave and lead like they know everything and have all the answers. But they don't. And I've watched some of them fail.

I, on the other hand, am clear that I don't know everything, and I'm okay with that. I don't worry that I am not always the smartest person in the room. I'm not the subject matter expert on everything, so I've learned to trust, guide, help, support, inspire, and motivate others to do their jobs to the best of their ability so that we can all be successful.

When we have business challenges, it's not always my job to solve them. Most of the time, it's my job to help others solve them. It's my job to empower people to do their jobs, not to do their jobs for them.

> **"I've learned to trust, guide, help, support, inspire, and motivate others to do their jobs to the best of their ability so that we can all be successful."**

When you combine all these traits and lead in this way, people will respond to and respect you more as a leader and feel more fulfilled in their own jobs and careers. Which is also what we all want and need as leaders.

Navigate Your Career a Level Up

One of the lessons I learned at a critical time in my career was that I hadn't navigated my career at least two levels above and more broadly across our organization. At that time, I worked directly for two men at different brands who had vacated their presidency roles, and both believed I was the right person for their position. They even recommended me for it. But I hadn't navigated my career above or beside them. I had only navigated my career as their direct report. This made my exposure limited and didn't help me get either position, despite the recommendations.

The reality is that when people are on an ascension plan, there is conversation around them and whether they are the right person for the role. It's important to know that those discussions oftentimes revolve around how well the person in question knows the people making the decisions. Those in charge need to know the candidate, their capabilities, and their attributes really well. You need to be aware of that and ensure you network well and with the right decision-makers so that when your name comes up it's an easy choice.

When I was coming up, there were limited opportunities to network at the right levels. I had to figure them out on my own. A big part of my ability to ultimately get my current role was the opportunity to talk to and work with our chairman and CEO very closely. Because I had been previously recommended for the role I so desperately wanted *twice*, and because he hadn't given it to me *twice*, I knew that the only way I was going to get a fair shot was if he worked more closely with me to see what I was all about, to check if I really had what it took, and to mentor me to achieve my goal. He had told me he didn't feel like I was the right person at the time. Both times. That was beyond disappointing, as you might imagine. But, again, I looked at the positive, which was that I now had the opportunity to have a conversation with him and work with him like I'd never done before. I was able to directly ask him what he felt was holding me back. And I continued to reaffirm to him that while I definitely wasn't happy with his "not yet," I was determined to turn his no into a yes. Which I ultimately did.

It took more time than I would've liked, and I experienced two missed opportunities when they presented themselves. It was frustrating, but I channeled that frustration in a productive way alongside my determination and persistence.

Did it knock me down for a second? Yes.

Did I express my frustration? Yes.

Did I do it professionally? Yes.

Did I channel it positively? Yes.

I learned later on that how I handled those situations made a big and positive impact on how the CEO perceived me and was one of many factors that contributed to the ultimate decision that I was right and ready to lead Celebrity.

It's More than Gender

Gender is the elephant in the room and such an important issue, so I want to address it in this chapter. Proving people wrong hasn't been about my gender, although there have been a few situations where my gender was met with skepticism. And that's understandable. I was moving into roles that women had never held before.

My countenance, the very soul of who I am, is positive and persevering. While I've worked hard, showed up, and ultimately "proved them wrong," the reality is that I've never run into any gender-related issues as I have climbed up the ladder. Any objections I've faced were due to my lack of experience and limited exposure to those who would ultimately make the final decisions, which caused them to believe I just wasn't ready or didn't have what it took. That's the point in time where I learned that you really have to run your own PR campaign. When I started out, I thought that, if I did a great job and got great results, I'd naturally get the promotions I wanted. I later learned that this is not always the case. I had to make sure the right people were paying attention to my success at the right time. I had to develop relationships with advocates who would help me achieve my goals. How will the right people know what you are capable of if they aren't watching? And, at the end of the day, it's not only important to do a great job but to also make sure that the right people know it and see it.

This can be a challenge for a lot of people, and in my experience, it can be a real challenge for women in particular. To "beat our chests" and let those who need to know that we are doing a great job and getting great results is absolutely necessary but not always easy or in our DNA.

I will admit that this is difficult for me, too, because I'm not a chest beater, and yet I have watched others around me do it quite well. It's not comfortable for me, so I have a tendency to go the other way. But what I've learned is that you don't have to be obnoxious or "in your face" to rise up the ranks—though you absolutely must do some level of self-promotion, or people will have no idea what you've done. No one else can do that for you.

You must be courageous enough to declare what you want, find out what you must do to get what you want, and then go about doing it. And then you must be courageous enough to ask why it might not be happening the way you want it to. You also must ask about and understand the gaps that might be holding you back. Again, none of this is easy.

> "You don't have to be obnoxious or "in your face" to rise up the ranks—though you absolutely must do some level of self-promotion, or people will have no idea what you've done."

Did it take longer for a yes to come than I'd wanted? Sure. And did I have to ask a few times despite being highly recommended for certain roles? Sure. But my yes came. And I have always believed everything happens for a reason, and, in retrospect, perhaps the timing was perfect.

Building My Credibility One Step at a Time

First, let's start with the fact that the cruise industry is a hundred years old, and it's changed significantly in the last fifteen. I was in sales and marketing for twenty-one years, in operations for nine years, and have been in my current role for almost ten years.

In the first two decades of my career, I was in areas of our business that were very gender balanced: sales and marketing. So back then, I never thought about gender as an issue. However, for the last nineteen years, I have been in roles that hadn't previously been occupied by women. And I went from working in a very gender-balanced area to working with mostly men. It's not unlike other industries, and—like other industries—things have dramatically changed in recent years.

All of the people who have sponsored, advocated for, and promoted me throughout my career have been men. Not because they were nice guys (though they were and are) but because I deserved it. Believe it or not, I never had a woman as a boss or mentor in my career journey. I have, though, had great women coaches along the way, and today I have great women that I do consider mentors who play a huge role in my life and career. They just came much later in my career and, for the most part, after I ascended into a very high position. But their presence in my life is invaluable and treasured.

So, it's only natural that, as I was rising up through the ranks, there came a point where I was being moved into roles that women hadn't previously held. It was a man's world—that's not a complaint or a criticism, just a fact. Thus the environment at that time could be a little tricky to navigate because it was different for me and also for the men around me.

There was oftentimes skepticism about my ability to fulfill these roles, mostly from the people who ended up having to work for me or beside me. Not only had women never held these operational leadership positions before—there sometimes were no other women in those functions at all. They'd hardly ever worked with a woman before, much less been managed by one.

So, I had a lot of work to do to build credibility and establish myself as a leader who transcended gender and subject matter expertise. I had to prove there were reasons why I was in the position, even though I'd never done some of these jobs before. I was managing and leading people who knew a lot more about their jobs and that part of our business and operation than I did. And they still do. I have never driven a ship or fixed an engine, and at that time I had never run a huge, global, and logistically complex operation. People had some hesitation about my leadership, and that was fair.

As time went by, however, it became apparent that I'd been selected for good reasons, including being able to drive cultural change successfully so that teams and the organization could continue to evolve, create better experiences for our guests and our employees, achieve better financial results, help others be successful at their jobs, make sure people had what they needed to get their jobs done, and support people the way they needed to be supported.

In my first position, I was more of a colleague and a direct report. And those I was working with were not sure I belonged there. They felt that I didn't know anything about operations—and in a way, they were right. They were skeptical that I would be successful. I had to think about how to prove them wrong.

I knew overcoming their skepticism would require more than just doing a great job and getting great results. What was I going to do to turn this skepticism around, to get these people on my side, and to earn their respect? **I learned that, sometimes, the right thing to do is to just put yourself out there and be totally transparent.** So, I sat at the front of the room and acknowledged that I knew they didn't understand nor were they comfortable with the changes I was making. Then I invited them to ask me anything, and I proceeded to answer every single one of their questions. That interaction immediately changed how I was accepted and perceived as their leader. People just needed to understand the "why" to come along on the journey.

I also learned that I needed their help if I was going to be successful. I quickly identified those whom I felt I could get on my side, and they fast and furiously became my advocates and mentors, helping me every step of the way.

I also soon learned the lesson that, at the end of the day, everyone wants the same things in a leader regardless of gender or subject matter expertise. It doesn't matter if the leader is running sales, marketing, an operations function, or a brand. Their people all want and need a leader who will stay true to the vision and strategy and support them in their jobs so that they can achieve their goals. We want a leader who has courage and who inspires us. Sure, you've got to know a lot about what your people do, especially when you need to give them guidance and support and help them make the best decisions to do their jobs successfully. I do that by asking and learning from those who do know—like I've said, I'm not, nor do I pretend to be, the expert. But ultimately, great leadership transcends easily visible credentials.

Phone a Friend

As I was learning and growing on my career journey, I was often faced with decisions where I wasn't certain which direction to go. And what I quickly learned in operations is that there is little margin for error. Whenever I was confronted with a problem or opportunity, presented with a recommendation, and asked for a decision, I would quickly realize that I needed help to make the right choice and would deploy one of my best leadership techniques, which I stole from the game show *Who Wants to Be a Millionaire?*—phone a friend.

I hope you remember that show. *Who Wants to Be a Millionaire?* was incredibly popular and aired for over twenty years. Contestants, hoping to win $1 million, were asked a series of multiple-choice questions. In answering the increasingly difficult series of questions, they could ask for help in various ways, one of which was to "phone a friend."

That's what I did, and I did it often. But a lot of leaders don't ask for help—and that's a big mistake because the only way to be successful is to have people on your journey who want to help you succeed.

Without self-confidence, it's easy to avoid asking for help. You might think that being vulnerable or admitting you don't know something will give people a lesser opinion of you. I cannot express strongly enough—and you'll hear me make this point throughout the book—that this is not true. I've learned that pretending to know everything is a huge mistake. I've learned you have to show vulnerability, and you have to ask for help. This is the only way to prove the skeptics and naysayers wrong rather than prove them right.

Funny thing is, when you ask for help, people feel invested in your success. They want to help you win. They feel honored and flattered. And they go the extra mile to help you. Think about it—does it get any better than that?

Head of Operations at Celebrity

In 2005, I went into my first operational role at Celebrity as head of operations. The complexity of our business can boggle the mind. Operations is everything that happens on board the ships, as well as what we do shoreside to build programming and experiences on our ships for our guests and crew. Operations is the biggest part of our business, and there are a lot of moving parts.

For instance, we run state-of-the-art entertainment facilities. We hire twenty thousand crew members around the world. We create all our own culinary experiences and our own menus. We work with tour operators all over the world who run all our shore excursions. We work with ports and governments around the world. We design and build our ships with the best shipyards on the planet. We maintain these ships—and so on and so on and so on.

There is the marine, or nautical, side of our business, which is responsible for the maneuvering, safety, bridge, and maintenance aspects of our operation that keep all the outer decks in meticulous condition. We have the technical side of our operation, which ensures that all of our engines and systems are operating and maintained properly. We have the environmental side of our operation, which ensures our systems and practices are followed and are above and beyond compliance at all times. There is the fuel side of our business, which manages our fuel consumption, fuel mix, and energy efficiency. We have gift shops and spas. We have logistics and containers arriving all over the world. We're buying product from everywhere around the globe. Our operation is huge.

People are often amazed at the complexity of our business. It's unbelievably big, all encompassing, and complicated. And it has to run like a fine-tuned Swiss watch. Everything has to happen on time and on schedule. Our guests embark, and everything magically happens for them. They don't realize what it takes to make it happen, and we all work hard to ensure it's as flawless as possible. And that's why our teams are so important. That's why their commitment and passion for our brand and our company is so critical.

When we were in the throes of designing and developing one of our series of ships, it was my first new ship introduction as head of operations, and I was definitely a little nervous. I didn't want to mess it up, and I didn't know the right questions to ask. I didn't know all the right processes and plans to put into place.

Not only was I new to the position and project I was leading, but I also had a new team, and I didn't want us to fail. It meant so much to us, and I remember thinking, "I have to do this well and I have to do this right—so who am I going to ask for help?"

I turned to one of our executive vice presidents because he had a breadth of experience spanning many years and was a close colleague. He had (and continues to have) a huge area of responsibility in the design and introduction of all of our company's ships and systems. He had run the hotel and marine sides of our business for many years. I decided that he was the friend I was "going to phone," and it helped that we were already working together very closely on this new series of ships.

I said to him, "This has to be perfect. This new class of ships is a very big deal for us. We haven't had a new class in more than ten years, and we really need this to be successful. I'm brand-new at this, and I honestly don't know what I don't know. I need help. Will you help me?" He didn't hesitate for a minute and said, "Absolutely." And that was one of the keys to our amazing success. I never would have been able to lead that launch in such a successful way if it hadn't been for him. And I wouldn't have had his help if I wasn't smart enough or willing to be vulnerable enough to ask for it.

I remember standing in the Grand Plaza on the first ship in the series when we introduced her. I looked around at this big, beautiful ship that we had built and designed and thought, "Oh my goodness, how does this all happen so beautifully?" Even I was in awe. Everyone loved this class of ships, and we delivered flawlessly. We received nothing but accolades from the press, our trade partners, and our guests. And I remember at that moment in time how it all became real for me. How I felt about the people who had pulled this off whom I get to work with every day. They are so fabulous. Most people don't understand the complexity of our business and what it takes to do this. It takes a village, and we give the word "village" a whole new meaning.

People had doubted if we could pull this off and deliver a luxurious experience with a series of ships that were 30 percent larger than the other ships in our fleet. But we did. Beautifully. Once again, we proved them wrong.

Change Agent

When, as I mentioned, I was denied two president roles despite the previous presidents' recommendations, our chairman at the time couldn't have been nicer. While I don't think he had any intention of offering me the position, he encouraged me to try. I didn't get the position, but I was moved over to our bigger brand and put into a higher role that included both hotel and marine divisions. This was a much greater role with a lot more responsibility. I would be running a much larger fleet, and I would be responsible for both parts of the operation.

Nonetheless, I was disappointed. I remember thinking, "Okay—I'm going to give this new position all of my positive energy, and I'm going to prove that I can be the leader of one of our brands."

That was in late 2012, and I had been with the company since 1985. And, although I didn't get the position, I was thrilled that our CEO was showing real interest in my career and development.

That's when he became a mentor to me. Filled with wisdom, he felt that the role he was putting me in was not only a lot bigger but would also help me get ready for a brand CEO role if that's what I really wanted.

As head of Hotel and Marine of Royal Caribbean, I was once again the first woman in the company to run both. And, once again, I encountered skeptics. After all, this was the first time I was heading up a marine organization, not to mention being the first woman to do so. They knew I had successfully run hotel operations, but that's an entirely different ball game, so there was a bit of doubt that I could run the marine arm.

Really, what did I know about it? How could I be their boss? I'd never captained a ship, never fixed an engine. But I consider myself a good leader, and as such, I know how to ask for help. I found yet another friend who was part of marine operations and someone they truly respected who would help me learn this new world. It didn't take too long for me to prove them wrong and to show that I was the right leader for them.

With every decision I made and every interaction I had, one at a time and over and over, I made changes and built a culture where we could be successful. I've always fully embraced my role as an agent of change.

Initially, all of what I accomplished was done without meeting staff face-to-face. Ninety percent of our employees are on ships, so they're far away from home base. It was hard for them to know me, to understand me, and to understand why I was making some of the changes I was making. Not easy for a new leader, and not easy for those being led. I learned that change is difficult for people, especially when things have been done the same way for a long time.

Nearly a year into my tenure in that role, I walked into our first captain and hotel director conference, where we were finally all together in one room. I always say everything happens for a reason, and this time was no different. Not all of the captains were able to attend the conference because some of them were navigating their ships. This created an opportunity for some staff captains to attend—including Kate McCue.

During one of the breaks, she came up to me to say that she was excited to have been selected to attend the conference, that she had been looking forward to meeting me, and that she supported the way I was leading and the things I was doing. During the conference, with all of the interaction I was able to have with her throughout our few days, I realized that she was very special and that she would make a great captain. I was just hoping it would be sooner rather than later.

If I hadn't been appointed to that position in 2012, I never would have met Captain Kate, and I never would have been able to hire her as the first American captain of a mega cruise ship and the first woman captain for the brand I would ultimately lead. That would have been such a missed opportunity for me, for the brand, and maybe for her, too. When I look at all that we've accomplished together, it's pretty incredible.

Another milestone that happened at the conference was that I pulled up a chair and sat down at the front of the room and said, "Okay, have at me! What do you want to know? What don't you like? What don't you understand? How can I help?" Everyone had a lot of questions, and I answered them. Openly and honestly. Then I brought up the rest of the leadership team, and we took questions together. We had this great open dialogue.

When we broke for lunch, so many people approached me and thanked me. I had changed their perception of me from the "unknown" to a leader who was accessible and wanted to support them. They saw the leadership team, the engagement and interaction. They learned what we cared about, what we stood for, and what we were trying to do. They got it. And they thanked me for the changes I was making and for the things that we stood for as leaders because they now understood and were completely on board.

That was a huge moment for me in terms of my leadership. I was able to once again prove people wrong about their misperceptions of me. And I was able to illuminate the value of positive change, especially in the operational environment of our brand. I learned that face-to-face, open, and honest dialogue

> **"Trust is at the heart of what is critical for a leader."**

is critical in leadership. Transparency and putting yourself out there isn't always easy. But it's critical to establish and build trust. And trust is at the heart of what is critical for a leader. Nothing happens without it.

After that conference, things were completely different for all of us. It was a turning point. And one year after that conference, I left that role and was finally appointed to my dream position: president and CEO of one of our brands. I will never forget the day that I made the announcement to that same group of captains and hotel directors at the following year's conference. One of the captains looked at me with tears in his eyes and told me he wished I was staying and that he was really going to miss me.

I thought to myself, "Wow—you've come a long way."

Patience Is a Virtue

As I transitioned into my new role as president and CEO of one of our brands, I had been in the company in various roles for thirty years. I had worked methodically and tenaciously during that time to do my best, to get the results I needed, and to stay positive, focused, and determined. And I had also learned to be patient. Nothing great is accomplished without putting in the time and gaining the experience you need—even when you face disappointment along the way. Many times, I talk to people in our company who express impatience over being in a position for a few years and not getting the promotions they want. I am not a sympathetic ear for them because it took me thirty years to accomplish what I wanted.

We don't always get the things we want when we want them. In those situations, the best you can do is internalize your feelings, respond from a positive point of view,

and change what might be holding you back—because those things are within your control.

Advocates and sponsors will support and promote you along the way. There will be skeptics, too, and you will have the opportunity (more than once, surely) to tackle the challenges with grace and prove them wrong. When you don't get what you want, it might not be because you've failed. Maybe you're just not ready, or maybe those skeptics just don't see what your advocates see. But they will. Because you'll change their minds in a positive way through positive actions.

It's okay to be resentful and feel discouraged but keep those feelings below the surface. Don't project them onto others. That will never help. If you are good at what you do, and you believe you deserve something better, it will come. It might be president or CEO or manager. It could be anything. Accept and embrace the skeptics, and then work hard to change their minds.

And as Oprah says, "I've been underestimated every step of the way, and it's so exciting when you can prove them all wrong."

4

~~~

Failure Is Success in Progress

"There is no failure except in no longer trying."

Chris Bradford, English author

When the chairman of Royal Caribbean, whom I asked three times before I got my "yes" for the CEO role at one of our brands, said in an interview, "I wanted to see her fail. I wanted to see how she handled failure," I realized two things. One was that he had obviously kindly blocked from his mind the most prolific failure of my career, and the second was that he had actually *expected* me to fail. He wanted to see how well I could handle failure when it inevitably happened. There were a couple of failures during the time I spent working very closely with him that helped him predict how I would handle failure in the position I so desperately wanted, so I obviously passed that test. However, the failure I remember the most, that had the most impact on me, and that was the greatest learning experience of my career happened many years before then.

Failure is inevitable; it's what we do with those "failures" that counts. The greatest minds in the world know this, and they know that true failure is only in not trying. Every time we rise up and meet the "failure" or manage the "mistake," we are actually progressing toward something greater. **I've learned that failure is a very important experience in your journey toward success.** I still have a hard time with this—I am not a person who accepts failure easily. Quite the opposite. Yet I know that without it, success is impossible.

My biggest, most colossal "success in progress" was launching a new brand in 2008. It was a failure of great magnitude for me—both personally and professionally. From a personal perspective, failing is difficult for me. And I never want to let people down. This wasn't a failure for just me—it also impacted people I cared about very much. My boss. Our crew. Our guests. Professionally, it made me question if I was right for my position. Maybe I wasn't cut out to be an operational leader. Some failures do that to you. They make you question *everything*.

My Epic Fail

In 2007, I had taken over hotel operations for one of our brands. Until then, I'd been in operations but only as VP of onboard revenue. It had been going great; onboard revenue was a continuation of and easy transition from my sales and marketing career. Going from selling and marketing to travel partners and consumers to selling and marketing to our guests on board had been a natural switch, and it had also placed me in the operational side of the business, which had been really important in bolstering my experience and career path.

Circumstances changed during my first few months in this new role as head of operations, and I was then thrust into a broader operational role because the leader who had been in that role decided to leave the company. While this was another great opportunity for me, I had only been in my position for eight months, so I did not have a lot of operational experience at that point in time. I was still learning. Another lesson I've learned: timing isn't always optimal, so you have to just figure it out and do the best you can under the circumstances. New to this position and now leading a team of people who were my previous

> "Another lesson I've learned: timing isn't always optimal, so you have to just figure it out and do the best you can under the circumstances."

colleagues in a culture that was still somewhat foreign to me, I was informed that we were starting up a new brand. And it was all happening "now." Talk about a steep learning curve. The proverbial frying pan to the fire.

We had purchased two ships from another cruise company, and we needed to start them up pretty quickly. And they needed a lot of work: extensive dry-docking—when the whole ship is brought to dry land so that the submerged portions of the hull can be cleaned and inspected—and significant interior refurbishment. We were on a very tight timeline.

With such narrow operational experience taking on this project, I had to count on the team of people I was working with and their expertise. They all assured me this was going to be fine and that they had everything covered and under control. I also had to rely on my colleagues in Marine and my direct reports in Hotel. Given their many years of experience and assurances, while I knew this was going to be a heavy lift, I thought I could do it. And I thought it would all turn out just fine. Boy, was I wrong.

We got to work. And pretty much everything that could go wrong did. I quickly learned that I was in over my head and that the collective teams I was working with, who had promised they had it all under control, in fact did not. And I didn't know what I didn't know.

Very little was going as planned, and very little was happening on time. It became clear the first of the two ships was not going to be ready for our guests.

I learned so much during this project. When you have to count on others so heavily for a successful outcome, it's especially crucial to surround yourself with, and be surrounded by, talented people.

I was in the midst of a situation that could be described as a perfect storm of things going wrong. The teams responsible for the readiness of the areas and the guest experiences did not meet the deadlines, and then there was me: the new leader who didn't know the right questions to ask and who naively trusted and took everyone at their word in an environment that was not built on trust, collaboration, and teamwork. In such an environment, successful outcomes cannot happen. The day before we were to welcome our guests, almost everyone left the ship. Some had to leave, and some chose to. I was the only shoreside leader left along with our crew, the hotel team that had to start it up, and the chief engineer who was going to continue to lead the work to get everything ready on the ship.

When it was time to set sail, many systems weren't working. Rooms weren't completely ready, and some items hadn't been delivered. Restaurants, crew, chefs, and housekeeping weren't completely prepared. Some furniture still hadn't arrived.

So many tried to help. And we were all so grateful to them. My boss was offloading trash and sweeping the decks throughout the night before guests were to arrive; another colleague was out buying pizzas at two thirty in the morning so the overnight team working so hard to be as ready as possible would have something to eat. Another team was also offloading trash and doing the best they could to help as the final hours passed by.

> **"I learned how important it is to have people you can count on and how very challenging it can be when you don't."**

The silver lining? I learned a lot. Most importantly, that the worst in people comes out in the worst of times. And, I learned how important it is to have people you can count on and how very challenging it can be when you don't.

Find a Way or Make a Way

I had to quickly pivot from the immense disappointment I felt. I thought, "Okay, I can't change any of this. There's nothing I can do to change the circumstances as they exist right now. But what *can* I do? How am I going to fix this?"

And that's when I learned that the best in people will come out in the worst of times. I looked at all the people who were still there—the security team, a staff captain (the second in command on the bridge), the hotel operations team, our crew, and me—and we decided we were going to rally and make it work.

There was only one other woman in any type of leadership position back then. I hadn't worked very closely with her up until that time, but she was another leader on my new team who knew everything there was to know—I just hadn't realized it yet. I remember looking at her at the time and asking, "What are we going to do?" She replied, "Don't worry. We're going to fix this. And I am not going to leave until we do." And we did. She became a key and trusted member of my team for many years. She's retired now, and I still miss her.

> **"I learned that the best in people will come out in the worst of times."**

She took charge of the staterooms and housekeeping, setting up the rooms and getting the flowers on board. She sorted through and took over our embarkation issues and processes. The rest of the team rallied, and we got the ship launched and sailing.

Was it a great launch? No. But I didn't give up. I stayed on board for six weeks to help get us into a good place. Seven-night cruises to Bermuda for six weeks. I didn't go home. I had to figure out how to make it better, roll up my sleeves, and get things fixed. I could not leave our team and crew. That never entered my mind. We were all in this together. I learned that, as a leader, you have to lead from the front. A leader never abandons the ship. You stay and face the music and help fix the problem. And from that experience, I gained more respect and loyalty during those six weeks than I had in my entire career up until that point.

Another big lesson I learned from this experience is that you need an experienced team around you. As a new leader in a new area, you won't always know what you don't know. And if you aren't hired as a subject matter expert, you've got to make sure the people around you are not only subject matter experts but also invested in mutual success, their colleagues, and you as a leader. The people around you and the culture you build as a leader are critical. We all need to be invested in the success of the organization and each other.

Most of the people who worked with me on that ship to help in our recovery during the launch of that new brand are still with me today—well over a decade later—in one role or another. We've been through the trenches together, and we have a lot of respect for each other. We've been invested in each other's success for many, many years. I have so much respect for them because they dug down deep, gave it everything they had, and worked their way through the mess. And their respect for me is because I didn't leave them on their own—and stayed for as long as I needed to. That spoke volumes to them about who I am. They had to stay. I didn't have to, but I did.

Out of the wreckage of that failure, I discovered an amazing amount of talent on my team that I was previously unaware of. That experience paved the way for great careers for many of them. These were all talented, committed, and dedicated people whom I might not have noticed if we hadn't gone through that together. And that has been the greatest gift of all. The happy ending of the story is that the brand recovered shortly after that, was eventually spun off as its own brand with its own leadership team, and prospered.

Scars and Recovery

There are still scars from that experience, however. Even recounting the story evoked difficult memories for me. Sometimes recovery takes a long time, but whether it's quick or slow, there are always lessons to be learned on how to become a better leader, how to avoid such mistakes in the future, and how important your team's talent and commitment is.

I hadn't understood the situation well enough going into it, and that's why the failure was so great. If I'd known a little more or had a little more time to build my own team, if I'd had more time to learn about an operation and a startup, it definitely wouldn't have gone so badly.

Good news is that we survived. But not unscathed. And coming out of such a failure was a long road, at least for me. The team and I often reminisce about that experience. We talk about it with affection. Because we know how difficult it was—but also how much we all grew from it and how we came out on the other side. We are all still standing, and we have made sure to never make those same mistakes again. We are better for having gone through it. We just never want to go through it again!

That experience also made me much smarter and wiser. I learned that I need to ask more questions and take nothing for granted. To trust but also verify. To ask what could go wrong rather than assume everything will go right. I now often ask, "What's the worst that can happen?" After that failure, I made changes and started bringing in people who understood what our mission was and who would help me build a stronger culture.

Starting up the new brand, I didn't know any of this. I was brand-new in the operation. I didn't know the questions to ask. I didn't realize how complex it all was and all the moving parts that had to be in place for it to work.

And I learned from that experience that siloed organizations will rarely succeed. Today, I am maniacally focused on collaboration and teamwork, and I do everything I can to create a culture where everyone knows what's happening. We discuss our problems and opportunities as a team, and we develop solutions as a team. Any time something has not gone well in my career, part if not all of the issue has been lack of communication and collaboration.

What Would Lisa Do?

From this failure, I created a set of simple, timeless, all-encompassing leadership values that I've now lived by for years:

1. Nurture employees
2. Play as a team
3. Foster open communication
4. Find a way or make a way
5. Do the right thing
6. Pay it forward

7. Walk the talk
8. Be simple and fast
9. Be better tomorrow than today

As a leader, I always lead from the front—positively. Sometimes people will tell me that when they have a decision to make, they'll ask themselves, "What would Lisa do?" They are counting on my leadership and following my example. It hit home for me after starting up the new brand that I needed to be someone my teams could count on. I didn't leave. I stood by their side. I helped them solve our problems. And I wasn't afraid to show vulnerability and tell people I needed help if we were going to get through this. **That was the first time I realized that showing vulnerability and asking for help was a strength and not a weakness.**

Culture, Culture, Culture

When I look at my leadership values, it is clear they were born out of this significant failure in my career. While I have always lived and led by these values, they were inherent, subliminal. After this experience, however, I realized these values needed to be front and center and that it wasn't just me who needed to lead by these values—so did every leader on my team and throughout our brand. They are also values I look for when hiring. They are in every job posting we have for our brand. I am often asked what I look for in candidates, and the answer is simple: Are they a cultural fit, and will they help us build and preserve the culture we have created? I've learned that it doesn't matter how much experience or competence candidates have. If they are not a cultural fit, they can't be a valuable member of the team and probably won't contribute to the team's success.

Another lesson I have learned is that culture is everything.

Establishing and maintaining a strong culture is pretty much the same as anything else; it takes intention, hard work, and heart. How much do you believe in it? Are you willing to give it everything you've got? And then, how do you surround yourself with a team who believes in and embodies the same culture you do?

What makes all of this even more complicated is that our ships are spread all over the world, so our leaders are as well. They are far away from the "mother ship," if you will. This lack of proximity makes things more difficult when situations go sideways on any given day for one reason or another. And it makes it a bit more challenging when you are establishing culture as the core of your leadership. But it's possible. And you do it one leader at a time, all the way down to every employee and all over the world. It feeds upon itself, it builds, it spreads, you see the results fairly quickly, and you enforce it with every interaction and every decision you make. This aligns perfectly with my favorite leadership value: "Walk the talk."

I've learned that our careers and our lives are formed by the decisions we make along the way. Regardless of the circumstances—good or bad—the decisions we make will determine how everything will eventually work out. And every decision has a consequence. That's why the options must be so carefully weighed.

One of my sisters is much younger than me. I've had responsibility for her from the time she was born, and she and I have a unique part sister, part mother, and best friend relationship. When she became a teenager, she began to make all the important decisions facing teenagers: whether to study or go out with her friends, what to do and not do with boys, whether to drink at high school parties or not. She didn't ask me for advice, but the "mother" part of me felt like I needed to give it to her. And that advice was not "Do this; don't do that." It was this: "These are your decisions to make. I cannot be with you twenty-four hours a day to watch what you are doing. Just remember that as you are making your decisions, ask yourself, 'Am I willing to accept the consequences of this decision?' It's your choice to make."

This is the same way I feel about culture and how I lead. Establish it, and then live it. Be purposeful and be consistent. People need to see you live it. And then, when you're not around, they'll know what to do, and then they will uphold the culture themselves.

I've learned that I have to visibly and constantly live my culture. I go to the ships so everyone can see who I am. They can see me walk the talk. I do my best to ensure that the team I surround myself with cares about the culture. It's important that they care about how people are treated and always treat them with respect.

It's okay if we're not perfect. We're human beings; we aren't supposed to be perfect. But if someone does something that goes completely against our culture, they must be willing to pay the consequences. Those are the choices we make. And we all hold ourselves and each other accountable every day for those choices. It's pretty simple. And that's why it's such a compliment to me when the people I work with tell me they ask themself "What would Lisa do?" when facing a decision.

Taking Risks

While not a stated value, part of any leader's job is taking risks. I will talk more about this in other chapters, but taking calculated risks is a big part of success. Each time I take one of these risks, there is always a bit of fear. No one can be 100 percent assured of success, but as a leader, you make decisions based on data, due diligence with your teams, experience, instinct—and then you go for it. An intentional recipe of components. Part of your role is that of a cheerleader, rallying your teams to head toward that positive outcome despite their own fears. It also helps to let them know how you feel. Let them know you are optimistic. But also let them know that you're not totally sure this is going to work—but there's a really good chance it will, and if it does, the reward is going to be great. Nothing great has ever been accomplished without taking some level of risk. One of my favorite quotes that brings together fear and failure is by Paulo Coelho: "There is only one thing that makes a dream impossible to achieve: the fear of failure."

Do I ever have doubts? Sure I do. Do I let these doubts hold me back? Absolutely not. Throughout my entire career, I have found myself in different positions where I didn't know everything and would ask myself, "Holy crap—can I do this?" And, every time, I can. I figure it out. Has everything been perfect? No. Life isn't perfect; careers aren't perfect. Sometimes you mess up, and it's okay. But none of my dreams would have been accomplished if I'd let the fear of failure outweigh my willingness to take a risk. I oftentimes say to my team, "The only thing standing in our way is us."

Your team is going to judge you on your body of work, not on one failure. They will evaluate you based on how frequently and consistently you take them in the right direction, with the right vision, doing the right things—not based on one mistake or errant idea.

> "I've learned that people aren't looking for perfect leaders. They're just looking for leaders. There's a difference."

I've learned that people aren't looking for perfect leaders. They're just looking for leaders. There's a difference. And how people feel about you when they watch you go through failure is more powerful than how they feel about you, or what they think about you, when everything's rosy.

Leadership is a game of percentages. Just make sure your percentage in the "win" column is high—because that's how you establish trust and credibility, and that's what gets your team to take a risk with you. Know that if you mess up, occasionally, it's going to be okay. And who knows what dreams you might accomplish if you just take that risk?

Flip the Pyramid

The leadership values the team and I live by are in no particular order. Except the first one, about nurturing employees. I consider it one of the biggest cultural behaviors I have championed. We have "flipped the pyramid."

The shipboard environment is very much modeled after the military. And your stature onboard is related to the number of stripes you have on your uniform. It's hierarchal. It has to be. The captain has the ultimate responsibility for safety and for all the lives on board. And, at the end of the day, their decisions or orders are the ones that all must follow. We have positions like captain, staff captain, hotel director, waiters, dishwashers, housekeepers, and cleaners. But, for me, it is more important for the captain to give the dishwasher respect than for the captain to expect respect from the dishwasher based on their position or the number of stripes on their sleeves. **You earn respect based on how you treat people, not because of your stripes or title.** And, if it weren't for the cleaner or the waiter or the person who makes the beds, those with the stripes wouldn't get a paycheck, and neither would I. The success of the brand depends on them. They are the heart and soul of our brand. And they deliver our award-winning guest experiences.

So, when you flip the pyramid and you hold people accountable, you strengthen the culture. That's how you get a crew who really cares and knows they are cared for. They feel valued. They give you the priceless gift of discretionary effort, and discretionary effort is a leader's secret sauce.

In the end, not all leaders are the same. We have different styles and motivators. But it's important we all lead by a set of values, that we take risks, and that we embrace failure and learn from it. As Confucius said, "Our greatest glory is not in never failing, but rising every time we fail."

And while this epic fail was the worst of my career, it was also the most important and positive in my development as a leader. And I rose from it.

5

Be Careful What You Wish For

vividly remember the day I decided that my goal and ambition was to be the president and CEO of one of our company's brands. It was 2010, and I was the SVP of hotel operations and working with an executive coach.

I've had a few coaches during my career and highly recommend them. Executive coaching is part of our company's ongoing focus on succession planning with high-potential officers. My coaches were all terrific and really helped me at various stages of my career and development.

In 2010, my coach was a man—the only male coach I have had. I will never forget him. He is wonderful and wise, and still a friend. As he and I were discussing what my future ambitions were so that we could determine what I needed to get there, he asked me if I wanted to be a brand president. At that point, I said I wasn't sure. He asked me why. I responded that I didn't know if that's where I belonged and if I would be happy.

I will never forget what he said to me, as it's probably the most profound piece of advice I have ever received. He told me the only way to have true impact is to have a seat at the table. And in that moment I decided on my new goal of becoming the president of one of our brands. He and I then began developing my plan to get there.

As you know, it took me a few tries, but as you also know, it finally happened. On December 6, 2014, I secured my president and CEO position. My dream job. I transitioned into the role from being executive vice president of hotel and marine operations.

It was thirty years into my career. I had been in various and advancing roles throughout the company during that time and I had a tremendous amount of experience and success (along with a few failures) behind me. I was ready. I walked into my new office full of excitement, optimism, confidence, and a sense of immense pride and accomplishment.

And then I clearly remember thinking as it all sunk in, "Okay, Lisa, here you are. Be careful what you wish for. What makes you think you are going to be successful in this position?"

Appointment as President and CEO

My first thought was that I wanted to be a badass CEO who would elevate the brand to transformational financial success. My second thought: How was I going to do that?

We've had some great CEOs of this brand who have enjoyed good success. But I knew the board expected better. That was what they and our chairman and CEO expected of me.

In that moment, I realized that I had to figure things out fairly quickly. While I knew I had a bit of time, I also understood there wasn't much of it.

To make a difference, we needed to build the brand in a different way. We needed to articulate the brand differently. We needed to be courageous, bold, visionary, and innovative. We needed to go for it, take some risks—and I needed to lead that charge.

I also knew that we had a new series of ships planned and approved by the board. The first of those ships was coming out exactly three years after my appointment. It was important to build the brand in a compelling way in the lead-up to these new ships. That was the only way we were going to be able to truly transform the performance of the brand. What was it going to take to do that? What were the tasks we needed to complete? We had a lot of work on our hands.

One of the things that was truly beneficial to me as I started thinking about the way forward was that I had seven years of experience with the brand. I had played a big role and was part of the major expansion of the brand with a previous series of ships, a group of five that we had launched from 2008 to 2012. I had been a key member of the executive leadership team of the brand during that time, and I had already formulated my own thoughts about what I believed could propel the brand forward in a meaningful way.

My sales, marketing, and branding experience were also a huge help to me—both back then and as I transitioned into this role. I realized that you can never have too much experience. It makes a big difference in your ability to hit the ground running and start making an immediate impact. I knew that my career up until this appointment, a thirty-year robust and winding path, had prepared me very well for this new role. My "Be careful what you wish for" thoughts began to abate, and I quickly transitioned into "Here's what we need to do, and let's get going" mode.

I knew we had to position the brand in a stronger way and that we deserved to charge more for the experiences we were providing for our guests. To do that, we had to determine which experiences were most important to the customer, and we had to strengthen and articulate those experiences in a more powerful way. I had to find the right team of people who were going to help us get there, and I had to continue to strengthen our culture.

Build Your Team

The most important thing any of us can do to accomplish ambitious goals and achieve success is to build a strong team. A colleague and I were both appointed to our current president and CEO roles of our two big corporate brands, and we both had teams in the positions we previously held. It's not uncommon for leaders to have key team members they believe are critically important to their success, and we were no different. We both agreed that we would each take two key team members with us into our new roles. To do anything more than that would have been detrimental to the areas we were leaving. That gave me a good start in building my new team, given all we needed to accomplish in a relatively short period of time. I took the next few months to continue to build the team who I felt could help us become what I like to call "a brand to be reckoned with."

We got to work quickly. I am not sure how many industries or businesses work at the speed at which we do. It's just the makeup of what we do. Regardless of the position you take on, including mine, there is no honeymoon period. It's full speed ahead. Full *warp* speed ahead. Again, the importance of experience cannot be overstated. The lesson I learned: Take your time. Get all the experience you can. It will never hurt, and it will always help.

We started tackling and strengthening our brand positioning, key onboard experiences, global sales effort, and pricing power.

Redraw the Balance

I was the first woman president and CEO of a brand in our company—and one of the first in the industry. I was also the first woman to join the C-suite in our company (there are now four). Being the first was a huge honor and well deserved—it wasn't just given to me; I earned it. I was thrilled to secure the role, but I'd worked hard for thirty years to get it. I'd navigated my way through the entire organization, building a résumé of experience and success. My appointment had nothing to do with being a woman. This was actually the third position I was appointed to where I was the first woman to hold it, though this was definitely the highest profile of the three. When I finally got there, I was determined not to screw it up. The spotlight was shining on me. With this role came huge responsibility. I was the first, but I certainly didn't want to be the last.

One of the things that is really important to point out here is that, unlike in some stories you might hear, there was overwhelming support for me going into the role. There was a groundswell of support from women in our company, regardless of the brand or the area of the company they worked in. They were cheering for my appointment and rooting for my success.

And it wasn't just women; it was also men. That's another thing I've learned throughout my career. Many, many men care about and create opportunities for qualified women to ascend into roles like these. They have daughters, wives, moms, and sisters. I can't tell you how many men have come into my office to show me photos of their daughters and to tell me that they can now tell their daughters they can do anything. All of this contributed to my overwhelming feeling of "Don't screw this up. Too many people—internally and externally—are watching. Don't let them down."

I've used this position and the influence it carries to move the needle and improve gender balance in areas across

> "Many, many men care about and create opportunities for qualified women to ascend into roles like these."

our operation that have historically been male dominated. Our industry is over one hundred years old, and the vast majority of our company's positions—and particularly STEM (science, technology, engineering, and math) roles like engineers—have historically attracted predominantly men. But as I entered my new role as president and CEO, things were changing, even on ships.

One of the first things I did when I came into this role was to build my team with an amazing man with whom I had the opportunity to meet and work with during my time running

Marine. As he began to help me in my new role, it became clear that we shared a passion for gender balance in our company and beyond. As a mariner and captain with two daughters, he wanted to show his girls that anything was possible. He and I got to make a big move very early on in my tenure as president of the brand by bringing Captain Kate McCue along with us for the ride.

I wasn't sure she would join us, but when he called her and asked if she would like to be the first woman captain on our brand and the first American woman to ever be the captain of a mega ship, her response was "Hell yes."

"You must use your position and whatever power and influence it brings along with it to create positive change."

And that was the beginning of what we have been able to accomplish. Since then, we have increased the percentage of women on our bridges from 3 percent to 32 percent with the help of yet another male head of Marine who believes gender balance is important in improving our business and our culture. Another interesting fact: only 2 percent of global mariners are women.

We have significantly more women leaders across our entire operation because they now have the same opportunities as their male counterparts. We have been able to lead our industry in this regard because we have been intentional and purposeful. You must use your position and whatever power and influence it brings along with it to create positive change.

To Thine Own Self Be True

I don't know if many of you who are reading this story are working in companies where you go through numerous assessment exercises. We use these kinds of assessments, and I have gone through more than I can remember. If you are familiar with the Hogan assessment, you know this is a very in-depth assessment of your personality that goes deep into your traits so you can understand them.

When I was reviewing the results of my Hogan assessment during the time I was running hotel operations for Celebrity in 2011, the coach I had at the time (the same one who'd told me I needed a seat at the table to make real impact) pointed out that both my "ambition" and "values" scores were, in his words, "off the charts." He had never seen that before, despite having spent many years in executive coaching and conducting Hogan assessments. He had seen executives score very high in both categories but usually a bit higher on one versus the other. Both of my scores were 100.

Over time, I've learned that when my ambition and values butt heads, my values win. It was always important to me that when I was finally appointed to a role like this, it would be through really hard work, a track record of success, the utmost integrity, and always doing the right thing—even when that wasn't the easiest option.

Everyone is always watching you. Many of those you lead will model themselves after you. I have had to make many difficult decisions. But I've learned that you can never be conflicted about decisions where integrity is at the core.

I have been disappointed as a leader when I have had to make decisions about people's careers not based on their competence or experience but because they have compromised their integrity and, in turn, the integrity of our brand and company. This is frustrating because their actions are in direct opposition to what they've said they stand for. And for me, this has been extremely disheartening as I trusted them to behave differently. I've learned that I cannot only look at results. How people achieve those results is oftentimes more important than the results themselves.

No matter how difficult a situation or how conflicted I might feel, integrity always wins. That's what the Hogan assessment uncovered, that's how I've built my career, and that's the compass that guides me in my decision-making.

Don't Rest on Your Laurels

You've got to keep innovating and evolving. You can't rest on your laurels. You've got to keep challenging yourself and your teams because there's always competition nipping at your heels.

Someone will always be copying something you've done that works, so being first doesn't last long—especially in my industry. I cannot tell you the number of times we have innovated something unique for our industry to gain a competitive advantage only to have three or four other cruise companies do the exact same thing in short order. People keep telling me that imitation is the sincerest form of flattery. For me, it's just irritating.

You've got to keep moving forward so you can continue to leave others in your wake. To be a successful leader, you've got to have the spirit of innovation within yourself and within your team. You've got to challenge yourself to think differently, do better, work smarter. As you navigate your business challenges, you've got to continue to change and evolve, staying ahead of the curve instead of falling behind. That is your best chance of dealing with the many different circumstances that can happen on any given day.

You've got to be prepared, which means you'll have to lay a strong foundation for success. And this isn't easy. This constant need to evolve and keep moving forward can be exhausting for you and your team. But it's critical. True innovation and big-picture thinking are rare. They must be cultivated and are a competence you have to hire against and continue to build.

Even the best leaders have a hard time with innovation. They have a hard time letting go of what they know or what they have always done. I learned a long time ago and constantly remind myself and my team that what got us here isn't going to get us there.

I have also found that creating balance on a team is really important so that you have the best ability to move forward and not rest on your laurels. **New blood generates new thinking.** New team members will challenge the status quo, always asking why. Experienced team members, however, are critical to maintain success because you need a base of knowledge to build upon. Too much of either is not the best or right answer or best team composite.

A big lesson of the COVID-19 pandemic was that the foundation you build is critical to resiliency. We all learned the world can go sideways at any time. A literal and figurative rogue wave can hit, and how well you're going to recover is going to depend on how innovative and strong your brand, team, and culture are as you try to energize the spirit of your organization through the best and the most difficult of times.

Being a Badass … CEO

When I became president and CEO, with many years of experience under my belt, I knew the expectations of the chairman and the board were high. Returning strong shareholder value was my ultimate responsibility.

I was determined to do just that, and I knew I had to do things differently than had been done up until then. Time for bold moves. Time for transformational results. And time, unfortunately, was not my friend. It rarely is. I needed to use all my experience and that of the team to start the trajectory of transformation and strong financial performance.

I needed to be what others now affectionately (I think) call me: a "badass CEO." What is a badass CEO? I'm guessing it's someone who performs well. Someone who is brave. Someone who takes risks. And someone who figures out how to change the trajectory and reputation of their brand.

During the first couple of years, I worked with the team to develop our five-year plan. As a new leader, I soon learned that nothing happens overnight. I learned it was going to take a little longer than I wanted. But I also learned perspective, which is critically important. No one expects immediate results, but people do expect results. At this higher leadership level, I learned that the accountability and scrutiny are in an entirely different league. And I needed the strength and the fortitude to be able to deal with that.

A big part of the successful turnaround for our brand was the new series of ships that were ordered before I came in to lead the brand. My boss, colleagues, team, and I did a lot of work throughout 2015 to completely redesign and reimagine the strategy for that series of ships. More on that in the next chapter, but that was the catalyst for the brand—not only because of the financial performance that series of ships would later achieve but also because of the halo it would provide for the rest of the fleet in both brand positioning and pricing power.

After two years of developing our strategy, doing our planning, repositioning the brand, changing our pricing structure and model, and incorporating bold ideas and change of direction for the brand, I was able to share our five-year plan with the board, showing a strong financial trajectory.

The trajectory was based on the introduction of this new series of ships along with the other changes we were making. It showed how all of these changes were translating into historic performance, which was the critical measure for them to assess my competence and success in the role I was in.

My ultimate success was overwhelmingly based on the financial performance of the brand. And that's how it's supposed to be. My team and I can choose interesting ways to get there. But the end result has to be strong financial performance.

That plan that I presented at that board meeting was the accelerator of everything that we have done during the time I was the leader of the brand. It drove us toward the financial results we've achieved. It drove the transformation of the brand itself. It enabled us to keep creating and innovating and improving our ships and our fleet and our experiences for our guests. It drove the stature of the brand within the company and the industry. It made us a meaningful contender and the premier brand within our competitive set. It enabled us to become a "category of one" in our industry, and it helped me become affectionately known in some circles as a badass CEO.

My aspiration for the brand was no different than the aspiration of any of those who held the position before me. What *was* different was the plan my team and I put together to achieve those aspirations. We envisioned the positioning and the potential of the brand differently. We thought about our target market, demographics, and psychographics differently. We thought about teams and team dynamics differently. We thought about passion, alignment, courage, and risk differently.

Nothing ventured, nothing gained. The team I brought together was aligned and passionate about our vision and our future. Nothing happens without that. And our colleagues in other areas of the company rallied around our vision and our strategy and helped us achieve our goals. I always say, "It takes a village." When you create and align around a bold and exciting vision with an aggressive ambition, with a great group of people around you who believe in you and what you are doing, the outcome can be even better than you ever dreamed it could be.

> "When you create and align around a bold and exciting vision with an aggressive ambition, with a great group of people around you who believe in you and what you are doing, the outcome can be even better than you ever dreamed it could be."

6

The Edge of Glory

**"A dream will always triumph over reality,
once it is given the chance."**

Stanislaw Lem, twentieth-century Polish writer

I am often asked, "What is the proudest moment of your career?" A difficult question, given my extraordinary and wonderful journey and all that I have been able to do and accomplish in my almost four decades in this great company. But to pick just one moment: launching the Edge Series of ships.

I will never forget naming day of *Celebrity Edge*: December 4, 2018. I was on the stage with our chairman and CEO, the captain of *Edge*, and the ship's godmother, Malala Yousafzai. Nate Berkus was hosting the event, and Andra Day was onstage singing "Rise Up." The feeling in the room was electric and magical. We were introducing a transformational ship and had a transformational woman as its godmother. Selecting a god-mother is a centuries-old tradition and the woman selected is the guiding spirit for the ship, its guests, and its crew. In my wildest dreams, I'd never thought that either of these equally monumental things would ever happen in my career. But there I was. And it had all started with a dream.

When I was appointed president and CEO of Celebrity in December 2014, it was an exciting time for the company. During my previous tenure with the brand, from 2005 to 2012, we'd designed and introduced the Solstice series of ships. Also, during that time, we were beginning to find our identity and solidifying our positioning as the brand was growing. Fast-forward to 2013, and Celebrity was once again designing and building a new series of five ships, the Edge Series, with the first ship to be called *Celebrity Edge* and delivered in the fall of 2018.

During that time, I was with our sister brand as the head of operations. When, in 2014, I came back to lead Celebrity, I was so excited for the future of the brand with this new series of ships on order. We were growing, and we were confident that we were going to continue to build upon our success. It was an exciting time to take the helm.

Right away, our head of sales, whom I had worked with as a colleague during my previous seven-year stint with Celebrity, insisted, "I want you to go take a look at the design plans for *Edge*." I initially put that off for a while for a couple of reasons. I believed the ship design was already "in the can" without much, if any, ability to influence it and was just about ready to be turned over to the shipyard to begin construction. I felt that going to see the general arrangement would not change the outcome of what had previously been done up until now. I was brand-new in the role, trying to find my footing, I had more immediate things to focus on, and the holidays were coming upon us quickly. So, I just kept putting it off.

But our head of sales is nothing if not extremely persistent—a big reason why she is so good and successful at what she does. So, *finally*, after numerous requests for me to "go and take a look at *Edge*," I finally did. It was in mid-January 2015. The general arrangement of the ship, its overall structural design, was pinned on the wall. The previous team had been working on the strategy and design for *Edge* for a year. And, as I'd originally thought, it was pretty much "in the can" and ready to go when I finally went to see the drawings.

The ship was fully designed, but what I was looking at was not in line with the thinking that the team and I had for the strategy of Celebrity's future.

The team and I had formulated a few important—but different—strategic imperatives for Celebrity, so the timing was perfect for me to take a look at the ships that were going to help us on our trajectory and path forward.

At that moment, I realized we needed to take a fresh look at the design so that we could further elevate our brand and build a larger customer base to be able to significantly increase our demand for the growth these five ships represented. We had on our hands an opportunity to transform the brand and the industry. It had been ten years since we'd designed a new series of ships, and it would be ten years more until we would introduce this new series of ships. The Edge Series had to make a much bigger splash. We had to think differently. Our future success depended on it.

Calling a Time-Out

The initial strategy for the series was to slowly sail all over the world, rarely returning to US shores. Accommodating approximately three thousand guests, these ships would be the same size as that of our Solstice series ships, which was the sweet spot for Celebrity. If we were going to build five of these ships, we would need to think in a dramatically different way about the first one to be launched and how it would transform the brand in a way that would be more appealing to people who hadn't cruised before, along with people who had cruised but with other brands. We would also need to maintain a high level of appeal for our loyal guests. Our target was the affluent vacation market. And our brand was nicely positioned between premium and luxury brands. We owned a unique and solid niche as a category of one. This series of ships had to further solidify this positioning in a powerful way.

Having looked at the design and knowing we had to think in a radically different way, my sales and marketing experience kicked in. As we were thinking through this, I asked myself: How are we going to generate a significant amount of buzz and excitement around this ship? How am I going to convince those who have not considered cruising (or cruising on Celebrity in particular) to do so on this ship? How are we going to generate the highest return on the billions of dollars being invested in them? How is this ship going to put Celebrity on the map and be that "brand to be reckoned with" we all want to create? As I considered these questions, I realized we needed to ask for a time-out.

I went to our illustrious head of New Build, to our head of ship design, and to our chairman and CEO, and said, "We're building five of these, and I think we can do this differently. The team and I have some different thoughts on this new series based on the direction we think Celebrity should go in. I know we owe this general arrangement to the yard, and I know a lot of work and thinking has been put into the current design. I know this isn't going to be easy, but I'd still like to take a time-out and think differently about this."

You build your credibility and reputation over your body of work over an extended period of time. This was a big benefit for me at this critical juncture; because I had been in the company for so long, and because I was the new leader of Celebrity and these ships were going to be delivered during my tenure, our chairman gave me his support, as did my colleagues on the New Build team with whom I had also worked for well over two decades at this point in time. Their support was critical.

So, we took a step back, a time-out, and we all got to work. Our New Build and Yard colleagues, architects, designers, and others around the company began the process of taking a fresh look at the design of *Edge*. Did we change absolutely everything? No. But we changed a considerable amount, as described just ahead. And what we didn't change, we enhanced. Made better and stronger. More compelling. More transformational. That's what's so wonderful about our process. The energy, creativity, and innovation build when we put our collective minds together and formulate our vision and ideas to create the foundation for the outcome we are looking to achieve. And everyone got into it. I soon realized that everybody, from our chairman down to the heads of our operational areas, was excited to take a fresh look at the ship.

We didn't just redesign the *Edge* ship; we also went back and rewrote the strategy for this entire series of ships, which included many aspects of consumer appeal, target audience, and lengths of itineraries. As we were thinking through the optimal itineraries, which included the necessary speed of the ships, our head of Marine at the time came into my office with some news that I wasn't prepared for. I'll never forget what he said: "Lisa, the ship is looking great. It's turning out to be wonderful. I think the strategy is spot on, but the ship isn't going to be able to go at the speeds we will need it to for the itineraries we have decided on. We need to add another engine." As I mentioned a bit earlier, the ship was originally designed to traverse slowly around the world, hardly ever calling on US shores. Our strategy had now changed, and the Edge Series was going to take over marquee itineraries with high consumer appeal that we believed would generate significantly more demand. To complete these new itineraries, the ship would need to sail at much higher speeds than we'd originally planned for.

Imagine my reaction to that news. Adding an engine to a ship is not an easy thing to do. And it's not inexpensive, either. It's not like redesigning a restaurant or moving the spa next to the fitness facility. Another engine adds an entirely new level of complexity.

Adding another engine was also going to impact certain guest areas because these engines are not small. I had to ask both our chairman and head of New Build to support this change. Fortunately, they did. I was very grateful for the support and involvement they had in every decision and designing every detail.

Our confidence was building that we had something very special going on. The good news about the time-out was that it did not delay the introduction of the ship. We worked incredibly hard to maintain the delivery schedule, even though it took us almost a year to make the design changes.

Everything we believed and all the experience we had up until this point gave us confidence we were making the right changes and decisions. That being said, it still took a bit of courage, combined with a certain level of risk, to ask for support for this new vision and direction.

At one point, I reflected on this time that had been so pivotal for me and Celebrity, and I wondered if the Edge Series had really turned out so different from our original intentions and if all the changes we made were really as dramatic and transformational as I remembered them being. Shortly afterward, I had dinner with our SVP of design, with whom I've worked for three decades. Since she'd been with me every step of the way, I asked her if my recollection of this period was correct, and, without hesitation, she confirmed that everything I remembered was 100 percent spot-on—and that these ships would never be what they were without our efforts. Coming from her, that meant everything.

Taking It to the Edge

At the same time we were redesigning *Edge*, we also got to work reviewing our brand strategy. We looked at where we were, what we'd built thus far, and where we wanted and needed to go. We needed to be absolutely clear around what we wanted to be known for, what our positioning needed to be, and what was most important to focus on to elevate our brand and guest experience.

Part of this process was writing the press release for *Celebrity Edge*. I learned from my boss that when you write a press release, it sets the direction and the vision that is going to lead your decisions in the right way. The compass, if you will. I use this philosophy for many of the things we do, not just for our new ships. As we composed the release for *Edge*, we used it as a guide not only for the design and experiences we were creating but also for our sales, marketing, and launch planning.

We studied consumer trends; we asked our guests and potential guests what was most important to them about cruising or to get them to consider a cruise. We found out they wanted to experience new cultures, go someplace they'd never been, eat excellent food, and connect with themselves and the sea. So that's what *Edge* was designed to do; we designed the ship to give them all they asked for. Their feedback became our North Star. We designed our staterooms, outdoor decks and spaces, and a very special feature called the "Magic Carpet," a cantilevered element that hangs over the side of the ship, to create a connection to the sea like never before. We literally took our guests to "the edge." Soon, the series name took on an entirely new meaning in how we thought about the ships and how they were going to make the guest feel. We incorporated as much glass and as many windows as we could into the ships' design. Everything became outward facing. We blurred the boundaries between inside and outside. So, for the first time ever, the project name became the name of the first ship in the series. *Celebrity Edge* stuck as the official name of the first ship introduced in the Edge Series. We just could not think of a more appropriate or perfect name for that first ship.

Everything about *Edge* takes you to the edge. Eden, for instance, a stunning venue in the aft of the ship, has more glass than does any other public space at sea. Our guests get to experience a multistory panoramic view of the sea spanning three decks that includes a specialty dining venue, café, and bar, plus entertainment. Our chaise lounges on our Resort Deck face outward toward the ocean instead of inward toward the pool. Our cabanas face the ocean, and our Magic Carpet offers a connection to the ocean and the destination in a much bigger and, well, magical way.

Naming the Ships

Naming ships is not easy. Probably hard to believe, but it's true. When the marketing team comes up with ideas and recommendations for names of ships, they need to create multiple names that fit the series. The names need to relate to each other and follow the same theme.

The Edge Series consists of five ships, the last of which, *Edge V*, will be delivered at the end of 2025. With great excitement, we chose four strong names from the list we had for the first four ships. *Celebrity Edge*, *Celebrity Beyond*, *Celebrity Apex*, and *Celebrity Ascent*—in that order. We could not decide on the name of the fifth ship, and since we had plenty of time, we just affectionately referred to that ship as *Edge V.*

In another first, when we sent out the press release announcing the Edge Series, we included the name of the first two ships: *Celebrity Edge* and *Celebrity Beyond*. Although we had never announced the names of two ships at once before, we thought it was a great idea. Why not? We already had the first four names. I soon learned that it wasn't such a great idea, and it would later prove that allowing yourself flexibility is always important.

Stretching the Limits

When my team and I got deep into the redesign of *Edge* and started moving and adding venues and experiences that we felt were important for the success of the ships and the guest experience, it became evident that these ships could afford to be slightly bigger. As I kept having that thought, I decided to be brave and say it out loud to the head of New Build. When I finally did, he told me he agreed with me. He had also thought the same thing at the beginning of the project. Come to find out, so had our chairman. Perfect. But he then told me we couldn't increase the size until the third ship. There just wasn't enough time between the first two ships to make that significant of a change. While a tad disappointed, I understood, and we moved forward with the first two ships being sister ships (exactly the same) and a plan to "stretch" the third in the series.

Soon after the *Edge* design was "in the can" for the second time, we got to work on the slightly bigger ship, and our heads of New Build and the Yard came back with their plan for the stretch. It was a stretch like none other before it—just as the Edge Series was like none other before it. This enabled us to add more space and redesign the most compelling and important venues for our guests, along with additional staterooms. This also allowed us to give more space to our guests on already very spacious ships. This redesign started to become so spectacular that we all started saying to each other, "I can't believe we have gone beyond what *Celebrity Edge* is. I didn't think we could do any better than that ship. This is beyond anything we could have imagined." Cue my epiphany that this ship, the third in the series, needed to be named *Celebrity Beyond*. So we swapped the names of the second and third ships.

Celebrity Apex became our second, while *Celebrity Beyond* became our third ship in the series. You can imagine the questions I got from our guests, our trade partners, and the press. Why did you change the names of the ships? I couldn't tell them, of course. We wanted to keep the stretch and the big changes as a surprise for well over a year. So, although it might have been better not to have announced the ship names so early on, when we introduced *Celebrity Beyond* to the world, they completely understood. Even to this day, the reaction to Beyond is "this is 'beyond' anything we could have imagined." Exactly what we were going for. I learned that I'm glad I trusted my instinct. It worked out even better than we planned.

Change Maker

Henry Ford said, "If I had asked people what they wanted, they would have said faster horses." In many ways, that's true. Especially if you are designing transformational experiences, like revolutionary new cars. **What you learn over time when you are innovating and creating is that customers don't always know what they want.** But you must know your brand, your customers, consumer trends, what challenges and barriers you are solving for, and what brand pillars are most important to you and your guests. You have to ask how you are going to attract guests to your brand from other brands, how are you going to convince people to cruise for the first time when they think cruising is not for them. You need to consider how innovation is going to differentiate you, your company, or your brand. And you have to create an environment that is conducive to transformational thinking and ideas to continue to push the envelope in ways that others never will. You also have to understand barriers people have that stop them from trying your brand—in our case, cruising with Celebrity, or cruising at all. And you have to pull out all the stops when you get the opportunity to convince them they are wrong. Once, when I was on a panel, we were all asked, "What is the one thing you would like to change if you could?" My answer was quick: "My goal is for no one to ever say again, 'Cruising is not for me.'" The Edge Series was our chance to do that. **I learned that we had to focus on a few key elements, and we had to redefine our competition.**

Design has always been a focus and brand pillar for Celebrity. The design on our ships is sophisticated and elegant, but in an approachable way. Given this focus and that we wanted to amplify our pillars with the Edge Series, I went to my colleague and good friend who is the head of design and asked her how we might really turn design for these ships on its head in a powerful way that had never been done before in the industry. As she always does, she said, "Leave that to me." And I did, because we have a strong history together. She is the best at what she does, and I knew she would find a fabulous solution. I just didn't know how fabulous it would turn out to be.

We ended up partnering with world-renowned designers Kelly Hoppen CBE, Tom Wright, Jouin Manku, and Patricia Urquiola. And then, to enhance this even further, we partnered with Nate Berkus, who helped us introduce *Edge* to the world. He brought strong validation for how special the design of these new ships was. I will never forget my first meeting with him. I flew to Los Angeles to try to convince him to partner with us. He agreed to the meeting but only gave us thirty minutes. We were there for ninety. I remember showing him the ship, and as I was going through the design renderings, he kept laughing. I asked him why, and he replied, "This is insane. This ship is beautiful. It looks like a five-star resort. Not a cruise ship." That was a big endorsement coming from him, and something we were so happy to hear. I couldn't have been more thrilled with his reaction and was equally thrilled when he agreed to work with us.

The design of the Edge Series catapulted our brand to where it is today and solidified our relaxed luxury brand positioning. We have been featured in *Architectural Digest* and defined by *Forbes* Travel Guide as relaxed luxury resorts at sea. This sort of validation of our relaxed luxury brand is all because of our amazing Edge Series ships and the equally amazing team of architects and designers who put their beautiful design expertise and passion into this project.

Why was this important? Because we wanted to change the perception of ships and ship design, especially in the affluent market. Bringing new people into cruising, people who might have had a negative perception of the luxurious nature of cruising, was our focus and critical to our future success. Proving we could deliver luxurious experiences at scale was likewise crucial to our success. With the Edge Series of ships and the significant growth it represented, we knew we needed to attract many more new and affluent guests to our brand. In other words, to use the old cliché, we had to go big or go home.

Going Big

The Edge Series ships are transformational in so many ways, but one of the most fundamental transformations and innovations is what we call the "Infinite Veranda." This stateroom design was not in the original designs or planning for the ship, and while these types of staterooms existed on river cruises, they'd never been done on an oceangoing vessel before.

Because being at sea and being on a river cruise are vastly different, the shipyard, architects, and our new build team had to find a company that could build a brand-new prototype of this type of "window" that could withstand and operate in the open sea. They had to redesign the exterior profile of the ship, which in and of itself was transformational. When you look at the exterior of a ship with balconies, you see them quite clearly as separate from the stateroom. They are literally attached to the side of the ship. When you look at the exterior profile of an Edge Series ship, however, you see a sleek profile that does not have balconies jutting out on the side of the ship. The profile is much more elegant with the Infinite Veranda—but the engineering is completely different and much more complicated. The engineering changes the structural support from endoskeletal to exoskeletal.

Why was this so important to us? There are very few opportunities in shipbuilding and design to add more space to a stateroom. The vast majority of the staterooms in our fleet have balconies, but the reality is they are only used by our guests about 10 percent of the time. Our guests and those who have not cruised before say that they would like larger accommodations because their room is a very important element of their vacation experience. The Infinite Veranda gave us the perfect opportunity to accomplish both things: a strong connection to the sea and the outdoors with their balcony, and a larger stateroom for their vacation. The Infinite Veranda blurred the delineation between inside and outside. It enabled us to make the living and bathroom spaces larger. When the window is open and the bifold French doors are closed, guests have a balcony. These staterooms take our guests to the edge of the ship in a way never before done.

> "When you go big like this with such a traditional element, not everyone will be a fan at first—and you have to be okay with that."

When you go big like this with such a traditional element, not everyone will be a fan at first—and you have to be okay with that. It took a while for traditional cruise passengers to get used to the change. We didn't give them a faster horse; we transformed the traditional stateroom and balcony on oceangoing vessels. This took courage and was a bit of a risk. But this became another groundbreaking innovation that put us ahead of the curve and disrupted shipbuilding and design.

When you position yourself as an innovator who wants to make waves, who wants to be a change maker and be transformational, if you're willing to be a little ahead of the curve and take a little heat along with it, you end up inspiring others around you to generate ideas and take risks as well. Our Infinite Veranda came to be on *Edge* because someone I worked with was inspired by our change-making vision for this series of ships and took the time to send me an idea that hadn't been done before that she thought might be really neat.

And it never hurts to ask for something again, even if it was considered and discarded previously. Timing is everything. It's part of my "never give up" philosophy. My village of colleagues, including our chairman, got behind these changes, which is another very special thing about our company. The spirit of innovation is at the core of everything we do. We set the bar. Always.

No, It's Not Aladdin

One of the features that was already part of the Edge Series when I stepped into my role and the project was what our chairman had named the "Magic Carpet." He loved the name. The rest of us weren't so sure, though, and we kept trying to come up with a better one. Ultimately, we couldn't, but that was okay—the feature and the name have been a home run. Another never-been-done-before architectural element designed by the amazing Tom Wright.

Even though the Magic Carpet was already in place, we all began collectively thinking about and reimagining it. It is the length of a tennis court and was originally developed to eliminate a pain point for our guests when we anchor off a port at which we cannot dock. Our guests have to take a tender (a smaller boat) to go into the port, which is a cumbersome experience for many reasons. The Magic Carpet was designed to become a tender platform that would be a much easier and more elegant way to get onto our custom launches (another transformational feature of the Edge Series) to go into port. When it's used as a tender platform, it's on deck one, but when it is not being used for tendering, which is 80 percent of the time, it needs to be stationed on a different deck. You can imagine how the engineering is extremely complex. We are oftentimes asked how we counterbalance the other side so the ship doesn't list, given the size and weight of the Magic Carpet. Another brilliant and complicated engineering feat by our chairman, head of New Build, Tom Wright, and the shipyard that I am always amazed by. They make all of this "magic" happen.

I learned during the planning for the Magic Carpet that every great idea can become even greater when a collaborative team with creative minds thinks bigger. Because the Magic Carpet cannot stay on deck one while the ship is underway, we have to station it somewhere else. But since it was such a special feature of the ship, we felt we should maximize our guest's ability to enjoy it. So, on deck five it becomes a seafood restaurant during lunchtime. On deck fourteen, late in the afternoons as we are at sea or sailing out of a port, it is an extension of our resort deck, where you can enjoy a cocktail and listen to the band as you overlook the beautiful ship and ocean at the same time. And the team came to me one day and said, "Lisa, we think if we could get the Magic Carpet to also be stationed on deck sixteen, we could have nights for our guests where we would serve 'Dinner on the Edge.'" We all loved that idea, so once again, we went to the head of New Build, who worked with Tom Wright to figure out how we could extend the ability for the Magic Carpet to be stationed all the way up to the top deck, deck sixteen. And they did. "Dinner on the Edge" has become one of the most popular events on board. Imagine dining sixteen stories above sea level, cantilevered over the side of this beautiful ship, looking at the sun setting on one side, the moon rising on the other, and the beautiful ship in between. Magical indeed.

Making Change Count

Now that we had the design of this beautiful ship, we had to ensure it would generate a lot of buzz and healthy returns.

That meant a compelling, courageous, and bold introduction of this new series of ships, like no one had ever seen before. Up until that time in 2017, I'd never seen or been a part of a "road show" like the one we put on for *Edge* in the lead-up to the introduction of the ship. Our chairman played a leading role in making this the "best ever" launch the industry had ever seen. He had a lot of fun with it, and his support, creativity, and "go for it" energy was contagious. Our colleagues in New Build helped with so much of what we planned. It was a ton of hard work, but everyone was "all in" and engaged, and I can say without question that this was one of the key reasons why this series of ships has been so successful.

We kept everything under wraps up until the big launch because this was such a big deal for Celebrity. The last time we had introduced a new series of ships was the *Celebrity Solstice* in 2008—and that introduction had not been done in a compelling way. This was a really big deal.

The series of events we had for this ship was nothing short of spectacular, beginning in Miami and ongoing in different cities throughout the course of the year before *Edge* was finally delivered. The chairman even had the steel of the standard balcony and Infinite Veranda sent from the shipyard so we could show how dramatic the reengineering was for the veranda.

We re-created it by building 1:1 scale mock-ups and showcased our Retreat experience, our exclusive "ship within a ship" concept for our suite guests, featuring an exclusive sundeck, lounge, and restaurant, all stunningly designed by our friend Kelly Hoppen. We'd never had this on a Celebrity ship before—another innovation for this ship and the brand because that's where hospitality was headed, and we knew the Retreat would be another big opportunity for the brand and the Edge Series to attract new guests. Today, we have retrofitted the Retreat onto the rest of our ships.

Press came from all over the world. The designers joined us. Nate Berkus hosted. Another "go big or go home" event that was part of this project. What was really special for me throughout it all was how passionate and invested *everyone* that I was working with was in this project and this series of ships. We all wanted this to be special for Celebrity and to completely change the trajectory of the brand and the perception of cruising.

> "If you can create that type of emotional investment in your project or your brand, you cannot help but succeed."

This kind of passion cannot be underestimated. It's priceless. It was our ship, and it meant so much to us. And, sure, all of the people involved were committed to doing well for us. But this wasn't that. It was so much more than that. My team *loved* this project. They were proud of it. They were invested in its success, and they wanted us to win—and win big. We all put everything we had into *Edge*. Magical. Epic. If you can create that type of emotional investment in your project or your brand, you cannot help but succeed.

All along the way, I was so grateful for the support from our chairman—for me personally and for Celebrity. Without his support, trust, and confidence, I knew none of this would have been possible. I didn't want to let him down. Not after all he had done for us. That was probably what drove me more than anything.

Claiming Your Worth

As part of our big launch, our PR team had scheduled embargoed interviews with the press so they could get their stories ready and publish them simultaneously with the big reveal happening two days later. I knew many of the press, given all my time in the industry. There was so much interest in these new ships, and I was very proud of the fact that for the two years we were designing and building this ship, nothing had leaked to them. That was truly a miracle. At last, we were excited and ready to share, and they were chomping at the bit to hear all about *Celebrity Edge*. It was the most talked-about new series of ships in the industry. I have to admit, I loved the mystery, intrigue, and interest.

The team put together a beautiful press kit with everything the media needed to write their stories, and I personally did all of the interviews and showed them all that was special about *Celebrity Edge*.

The presentation included the stunning visuals of all the spaces and the transformational and innovative features of the ship. They were blown away. This was primarily travel press, long-term seasoned and somewhat jaded reporters who had seen everything in our industry—and they were left speechless by *Edge*.

They had the same reaction as Nate Berkus when I showed him the ship under NDA: *It's amazing. I knew it was going to be special. I didn't realize how special. I can't believe this is a ship. You*

have outdone yourself. You have transformed the industry. Wow.
These were just a few of the things they said, but I could tell
by their reactions we were onto something really big. Bigger
than even we knew. And even better than we thought. Then
the press asked me another question: "What's the starting rate
for the ship?" And when I told them, each one of them asked,
"That's all?"

Which really got me thinking: We've got one chance to do
this right. We've got one chance to introduce the most transformational ship in the world, and this is it. Here I am talking
to the jaded travel press. They've seen everything and know
everything about cruising. They are awestruck by this ship, and
their reaction to the starting price is "That's all?"

This was two days from launch. Two days from opening
for sale. All sailings and prices were in the system. The team
had worked so hard getting it all done and ready for launch
day so we could prepare for the onslaught of bookings we were
expecting. But everything inside of me said, "We've got to raise
our prices before we open for sale. We've got to go for it." So,
after the interviews were done, and after I soul searched and
came to that final decision, I went for it. I called in our head of
marketing, our head of revenue, and our head of sales. I told
them about my interviews. I told them the reaction to the ship,
and I told them the press' reaction to our starting price, and I
said, "Team, I don't think we're charging enough for this ship.
I want to raise the prices."

The first response came from our head of revenue. "But all the pricing is in the system. Do you know what it would take to change it?" Followed by, "It's already priced significantly higher than any of our other ships. That's too much." Then our head of sales jumped in and said, "LLP"—my initials—"I think that's a big mistake. These prices are already high. You are setting us up for failure." Our head of marketing was new, so he hadn't been able to formulate a strong point of view. He just said, "It seems a bit crazy, but I'm new, so what do I know?" Not a huge vote of confidence from this critical team that had to price, market, and sell this ship. But what I learned in that moment is that sometimes you just need to be the boss. I don't like those situations. I want everyone "all in" and believing in what we are doing and the decisions we make. But that's not always possible. I had to trust my instinct and what I truly believed based on the conversations I'd had and the reaction to the ship. We had something really special here. We could not squander this opportunity. If I ended up being wrong, I would make a pricing adjustment. But I really didn't believe I was. So, I told them that I appreciated their point of view, but I wanted the prices raised and told them by how much. Our head of marketing said okay and left to change the messaging to include the correct price. The head of revenue stormed out of my office and didn't speak to me for three days, and our head of sales, who was the last to leave said, "Okay, you're the boss."

I knew this was a huge amount of work for the team. I knew they weren't happy and that they disagreed with my decision. But two days later, we launched the ship—and bookings came in like crazy. Like nothing we had ever seen before. And at the new rates we were charging. We all had to pinch ourselves to make sure it was real. Then, we started raising prices even further where we could because the demand was so strong. We all celebrated and high-fived and relished the moment.

> **"It's really the trust your team has in you as a leader that will ultimately determine if they are going to stick around and go along for the ride."**

This goes back to building your credibility as a leader one decision at a time, one risk at a time. My team hadn't agreed with me, but ultimately, it all worked out. While they might not have agreed with me, they trusted me. So, they went along with it. Although you'll build your credibility through your body of work and the decisions you make over time, it's really the trust your team has in you as a leader that will ultimately determine if they are going to stick around and go along for the ride.

The other thing I remember about all of this is how badly I felt when my team left my office after hearing my price-increase request. Why didn't they see what I did? Why didn't they believe what I believed? Our belief systems are built on the experiences we have over time. Their beliefs, based on their experience up until that point, were that we could not charge those prices because we never had before. They were skeptical. But I learned long ago that we cannot let history dictate our future and that our future is ours to write. And write it we did.

7

≈≈≈

The Comeback Will Be Stronger Than the Setback

"Turn every setback into a comeback."

Kobe Bryant, American professional basketball player

When the COVID-19 pandemic caused the world to take a time-out in March 2020, cruising stopped, and our industry shut down. We would not be able to sail again out of a US port until June of 2021: fifteen months later. While we tried everything possible when working with our industry colleagues and US government officials, nothing we did was going to change that outcome.

This wasn't a purposeful time-out like the one we took when we redesigned *Edge*. This was an industry time-out. While COVID impacted business around the globe, and hospitality in particular, it didn't impact any industry as much as it did the cruise industry. There was nothing we could do about it but accept it and do our best to get through it together.

The executive committee of the company was doing everything it could to get us through this time. The initiatives were endless. Our CFO and his team worked to ensure we had the financing we needed to sustain us. Our chairman worked with other cruise company leaders, health experts, and government leaders to keep the dialogue going in the hope that we would eventually be given the green light to start cruising again. It was a long and arduous time. When we shut down in March, we were sure we would start back up again in the summer. Didn't happen. Then, we thought, by the holidays. Didn't happen. The winter, then. Didn't happen. Then, in June of the following year, it finally happened. But those fifteen months were a time that I never thought I would experience in our industry or as a leader. For fifteen months, I knew I had to somehow keep people inspired and motivated to continue moving forward, hopeful and confident that this would eventually end and we would be back. I did not want them to wallow in the uncertainty and fear of what we were facing. I felt a big responsibility to rally my team, to understand what they were going through, to keep them confident, energized, and optimistic that we would get through this, even on those days when I wasn't so sure myself.

Never Let a Good Crisis Go to Waste

During our shutdown, our boss repeatedly reminded us of the famous Winston Churchill quote I mentioned in chapter one: "Never let a good crisis go to waste." I took that advice to heart and thought about how to apply it to my team and Celebrity. What was I going to do to assure that this crisis wouldn't go to waste? Looking at our situation in the most positive light, which wasn't easy to do, I decided to once again search for the silver lining in the COVID-19 cloud. I decided to think about what we could do during this unplanned time-out to reflect on our brand and how we could strengthen it so that our comeback would be stronger than our setback.

Few businesses ever have time to reflect on priorities and reimagine their brand the way we did due to the pandemic. In a steady state of business, we are always so busy driving, selling, hitting KPIs (key performance indicators), taking care of customers, keeping the ships full and our crew happy. We push every day without stopping. We work at warp speed. Sure, we take time to develop our five-year strategic plan. We formulate annual operating plans and KPIs, create budgets and revenue plans. However, when things are normal to thriving, there's usually not a lot of deep reflection going on.

You plan; you watch the business environment; you pivot; you make sure to hit your revenue and volume. You ensure the operation is running smoothly, the ships are maintained appropriately, e-commerce is coming in, investments are being made in the right areas, and, of course, that you have new ships on order and you bring them into the fleet one at a time. All of this goes on and on day in and day out—the amount of activity is incredible.

It's exciting, fun, wonderful. Of course, there are challenges, but there are also so many special moments to celebrate. For me, it had been this daily striving and driving to help build the brands within our company for thirty-five years that fueled me. And then, wham! Global shutdown. And life as we knew it stopped.

We were busy. Incredibly busy—but doing things necessitated by the shutdown, not the things we'd been doing on a daily basis for years. We were doing things we'd never had to do before, like getting all of our guests and crew home, laying up our ships (preparing our ships to be idle), and ensuring we were motivating skeleton crews of one hundred on each ship when we usually have 1,400 crew members and three thousand guests on our ships at any given time. Our ships were now dormant, sitting off ports around the world.

We were staying connected like so many others on screens in our homes, getting through the long shutdown completely separated from each other.

We were waiting for the call that we were coming back, but that call didn't come. It was weeks, months, and then well over a year before it did. It sunk in one day that "We just don't know how long it's going to be before we can come back."

As a leader, what do you do? Our teams were dealing with so much. Canceling cruises and guests' vacations, refunding money, dealing with thousands of calls and questions, staying in touch with our travel partners who were also going through so much themselves, and trying to stay connected to each other as best we could—all over the world. After all the years of positivity, of fulfilling dreams and making people happy, of building revenue and profitability and feeling great about how things were going—all of a sudden, all of that stopped. And worse, there was nothing we could do about it. Everything was totally out of our control. This was just unacceptable to a driver, someone who is always moving forward, like me.

I remember sitting there, wondering when we were going to come back. I knew we would, but not knowing exactly when was exhausting and a little scary. And if I felt that way, I could only imagine how my team, our shoreside employees, and our crew all over the world felt. They were exhausted from all of the issues around our displaced guests and canceled cruises.

As the months passed, I could see my team's hope and confidence fading. I knew that we couldn't keep having the same conversations; we couldn't keep wallowing in the negative situation we were currently in. And that's when it hit me. We needed to focus on the future. We needed to focus on the comeback.

#HopeFloats

One of the places where many cruise ships were anchored during the shutdown was off the Bahamas. One of these ships was *Celebrity Edge*, and Captain Kate McCue was at the helm. Like all of us, the captains of the ships were going through a very difficult time, with only about one hundred crew members onboard. That is devastating when you think about it. Captain Kate decided that she wanted to do something that would give hope to the ships she was surrounded by. She had an idea and communicated with all of them that at 5 PM every day, every one of the ships anchored there from many different cruise brands would sound their horns in solidarity and hope. She created the hashtag #hopefloats. And that was their rallying cry for fifteen months.

"Find a rallying cry for your team to coalesce around."

It was perfect. I decided I would also use her hashtag as our rallying cry. Another lesson I've learned: find a rallying cry for your team to coalesce around. I was determined that we would be stronger, better, and more confident coming out of this terrible setback than when we went into it. To stay focused on the positive, I knew we needed a project to focus on that would set us up for future success and give us a positive and motivating reason to come to work every morning.

Before our shutdown, we had a project underway. We had begun working with a luxury brand strategist to help us validate our brand positioning and refine our long-term strategy. We had five Edge Series ships coming into our fleet, which represented significant growth for us. We engaged this luxury brand strategist to help us strengthen our brand positioning by enhancing our offerings and our messaging. We wanted to ensure we were set up for success for the future.

Despite our circumstances, I worked with our head of HR, and we reengaged on this project because I believed it would make a big difference to our team in the immediate term and our brand in the longer term. A word of advice: Don't let your current situation jeopardize your long-term strategy and future. The day I announced that we were going to spend our time-out in this way was the day that changed everyone's mindset. Our focus completely shifted. The team was excited. Energized. I remember noticing how good that felt. I hadn't seen them that way in months. As a leader, I remember thinking that this was how it's supposed to be. This was how we are supposed to feel. And while so many others in our industry were still enveloped in the negativity of our situation, my team

> "A word of advice: Don't let your current situation jeopardize your long-term strategy and future."

and I were not. We were focused on our future. We knew that our comeback was going to be stronger than our setback. We were determined to make it so.

We got to work with the luxury brand expert to help us better understand the more affluent customer, how our brand and experience did and did not address their needs, if our positioning was strong and on target, and how we might expand our target customer to ensure we would meet our future growth in the most profitable way possible. We looked at our brand to consider if there were ways we could reposition to attract more of our most desirable customers. We explored how we could further differentiate ourselves and set ourselves even farther apart from our competitors.

New Luxury

As we challenged ourselves on how we wanted to use our time-out in a positive and productive way to make our brand stronger, we couldn't have been more pleased with the outcome. We ended up making deeply meaningful changes based on our modified strategy.

One of the key outcomes that we wanted from this project was to be able to compete with four- and five-star land-based resorts, not just other cruise lines. The reality is that cruising makes up a very small percentage of the travel industry. To truly grow our customer base, we had to convince travelers heading all over the world and staying in luxury land-based resorts that they needed to go to those same places on our resorts—which just happened to be floating. And we needed to significantly grow our customer base with a 74 percent increase in the size of our brand with the five Edge Series of ships. I've learned that you need to continue to reassess your competition and your brand to ensure you are optimizing your potential.

We had two meaningful epiphanies during this time, which led us to two changes in our go-to market strategy. First, while everyone else was talking about millennials and Gen Z, we recognized that our sweet spot was Gen X. We learned as much as we could about them during this time-out, and we grew more and more excited about them. We found out they were the perfect age for our brand that attracts a very high percentage of boomers. We wanted to continue to lower our average age of guests, and Gen X was the perfect generation for us to target to make that happen. They are a large percentage of the population. They have families. Their children are older. They want to visit the world. They are secure in their professional lives, they have disposable income, and they care about the same things we do. Gen X is known as the forgotten generation. Everything you will read will suggest that's true. They were forgotten even by us—but not anymore. We also realized that by focusing our messaging and marketing on them, we were attracting boomers, too, who are very important to us, as well as millennials, who are also a growing percentage of our guest mix.

We also studied and did research on the luxury traveler and what they are looking for. This was the catalyst for probably the most significant change we made during this time: launching our all-included pricing strategy. Luxury guests want simplicity. They want everything included in the price they pay. That's more important to them than a low price. We looked at the three things that everyone who vacations with us wants included in their cruise fare: tips, Wi-Fi, and beverages.

Lastly, we nuanced our positioning and used "new luxury" as the descriptor of our experience. We have since edited this to "relaxed luxury," but in all cases we want to ensure that we are not perceived as traditional luxury. We are more approachable and comfortable than traditional luxury. The definition of luxury has changed. We are not pretentious. We offer luxurious experiences at scale. By doing this, we have been able to become a category of one. **It's important to stand out in a unique way, especially in an industry that is still young and not yet well understood by consumers.**

Our Pandemic Baby

Much has been said about pandemic babies. There were many! We had one as well. *Celebrity Apex* was delivered virtually, the day the shipyard turned the ship over to us to operate, at the end of March 2020, two weeks after we had shut down, and she sat in the shipyard until September. She had nowhere to go. Our 1,400 crew members were sent home after this industry-first virtual-delivery celebration. And there *Apex* stayed for five months. In September 2020, we brought her back to the United

States because we were certain we'd start back up in December for the holidays. Soon, *Apex* was anchored off the Bahamas with many other Celebrity ships, including her sister ship, *Edge*. But the holidays came and went, and we still weren't sailing.

In the spring, we decided that if we couldn't start up in the United States, we would start our ships up in other countries and parts of the world that were reopening to tourism and cruising. Greece was one of the first countries to open, so in April we sent *Apex* to begin cruising in the Greek Isles in June. Fourteen months after delivery, she was finally welcoming guests. It was a very emotional time for all of us—our office team, our officers and crew, and our guests. Many tears of joy were shed. *Apex* was finally sailing, and it was a happy time for all of us. After her season in the Greek Islands, *Apex* headed back to Florida in October of 2021 to begin her Caribbean season. But before that, we had to do something very important that we had not yet done: name her. A ship naming ceremony is very special. It's the day the ship is officially welcomed into the fleet and is celebrated with great fanfare, including the ceremonious christening of the ship by the godmother and the breaking of a champagne bottle against the ship's hull. In early November of 2021, 581 days after she was originally supposed to be named, we had a beautiful naming ceremony. Another emotional time for all of us, especially the captain and crew of *Apex*. At long last, they had their day in the sun. What was also very special was the audience and how happy they were to be celebrating again. The joy and appreciation for where we had finally come to was palpable. And it felt really good. As human beings, we want to celebrate and be connected to humanity. Living shut down and shut off goes against human nature.

Green Light ... Go!

Closer to home and also in June, *Celebrity Millennium* began sailing out of St. Maarten in the Caribbean. Earlier that spring, we had started believing that the CDC (Centers for Disease Control and Prevention) was going to give us the green light to sail again. We knew there would be very stringent protocols, but we also felt like we were finally seeing light at the end of the tunnel. We had no idea when this would actually happen, but you could sense the tide was turning based on the ongoing dialogue the industry was having.

So, we got ready. That wasn't as easy as it sounds. We had to find vaccines for our crew, and we had to find a way to get them vaccinated before they joined the ship. We had to house them in hotels and then bring them on board so we would be ready to go when the time came. Our company wanted to be first and had the foresight to put us in a position to do just that. Our teams got to work. It worked out that *Celebrity Edge* would be the first ship to sail out of the United States when the time came. And Captain Kate would be at the helm.

Finally, the call came, and the industry got the green light to sail—but only our company was ready. And, as planned,

Celebrity Edge went first, and a ship from our Royal Caribbean International brand would sail a few days later. Because of our amazing shoreside and shipboard teams, our company's brands were fully ready to go. It was June 26, 2021. Our crew was excited. Protocols were in place. We sailed with a smaller number of guests during the start-up, and the CDC was there to inspect everything, and they were satisfied with all we were doing.

Prior to setting sail, our head of PR called me and told me that there were many members of the press who wanted to sail on this first cruise. Naturally, there was a tremendous amount of interest in being on the first ship out of a US port since the shutdown. As you may recall, the press was not kind to our industry during the pandemic. It was not surprising that so many wanted to be on this first cruise, including all the major news outlets and morning shows. Our head of PR asked me how I felt about the press joining us, and it would have been easy and understandable for me to say no. But I also knew how big this moment was—for our industry and for Celebrity. I thought for a minute, looked at her, and said, "Bring it on."

Was it a risk? Absolutely. This scrutiny was going to be excruciating, especially for our crew. The press would be watching and reporting on everything. This could be a home run or a disaster. We could succeed or we might fail. There was so much more to coming back than we were used to with the new regulations. And the pandemic was still very much with us. But, like I said in chapter four, nothing great comes without taking risks. Just make sure your risk is calculated. You have to base your decisions on everything you know combined with everything you believe and your instinct. And, when I looked at the opportunity in front of us, while I knew it was a risk, I also knew what the reward could be. And I knew what it could do for our brand and our industry.

But mostly, the reason I said "Bring it on" was because of another lesson I'd learned: I had to trust and have confidence in my team. I knew what they and so many others in our company had all gone through to get to this day. I knew they had it under control. I trusted Captain Kate and her entire hotel and marine crew. I knew they were ready and proud, and I knew they were not going to let us down. I knew they were going to shine and prove to the world we were back and the safest place in the world to take a vacation. I knew our guests were excited and couldn't wait to get on board. I trusted that our operations team had done everything needed to prepare us. I trusted all my colleagues around the company who'd helped. I knew everything was in place to make sure everyone was going to have a great cruise and that they were going to be safe.

"When your team knows they have your trust and confidence, they, in turn, are not going to let you down."

When you have that level of trust and confidence in your team, and they look at you and ask, "Should we do it?" you say, "Yes!" When your team knows they have your trust and confidence, they, in turn, are not going to let you down.

The cruise was a resounding success. The reviews and write-ups we received were incredible. We were everywhere. Cruising was back, and Celebrity led the way.

This was bittersweet for me, though. For my team and for Celebrity, it was the most extraordinary day. It was so positive, and everything worked out so beautifully. We were back—and stronger than ever. But as much as I wanted to be with my team, I was not there. I was in my hometown in Massachusetts because, coincidentally, on that same day we had scheduled my sister's burial at sea. After all we had gone through, and on the very day we became the first ship to sail out of a US port, I could not be there.

But there was never a question in my mind as to where I was going to be that day. Once again, joy intersected with terrible sadness. Funny how that happens. My boss told me I was where I needed to be. He told me not to worry about a thing. He told me he had this. He was there alongside my team on that very special day, and I was so grateful to him for that. And, as expected, my team did a great job. And they knew I was there in spirit.

As a leader, I learned something from this experience: **You need to build a strong team so you don't have to be there.**

That's when you know you have been successful as a leader. It needs to all go well whether you are there or not. I didn't have to be there for the reopening to be successful. My team knew exactly what to do to make it spectacular. The culture is strong, the passion is incredible, their professionalism is second to none. That day wasn't about me. It was all about them. And they shone brightly.

We're Back!

After that sailing in June, we were full steam ahead in reopening our ships. In the following twelve months, we started up our entire fleet of fifteen ships. Unheard of. In the past and throughout my career, the cadence of opening ships was with the new builds and that was, at most, one ship per year. Maybe one every eighteen months. Never in my wildest imagination did I think we would or could reopen fifteen ships in twelve months. A testament to the amazing team of people all over our company. Momentum was building, and we were slowly but surely coming back. By June 2022, we started up the last ship in our fleet. Today, we have steadily built our business back, and our ships are full again.

Bringing the ships back was such a boost to our optimism, our energy, our excitement, and our belief in the future. And when someone asks me, "What is the best thing about coming back?" I can confidently say, "Bringing our crew back to work."

Every time I've been on a ship since the reopening, our crew members have come up to me with tears in their eyes, thanking me for all I did to get our ships up and running again so they could return to work—but they were my inspiration every day. There were so many reasons we needed to get back into business and to get our ships back into service. But our crew was at the top of my list.

At the time of this writing, the worst of the pandemic is finally behind us. Normalcy is pretty much back. People want and need to travel, and there is significant pent-up demand to visit all the beautiful places in the world that people have not been able to visit for a few years.

When I was standing on the stage for the naming of *Apex*, I remember the feeling of the crowd. They were jubilant. They were so excited because we were finally celebrating not only *Apex* and Celebrity but also something so special and

> "While a pandemic or something else might knock you down, with resilience, no one can count you out."

so meaningful that we all had taken for granted: our ability to sail about the world freely and without fear. Everyone in the audience was rejoicing that we were coming back together after so many months of isolation and confinement.

Today, the world is open. Ships are full again, crews are back to work, and we are looking through the windshield—not in the rear-view mirror. In April of 2022, we introduced the most spectacular ship in the world, *Celebrity Beyond*, to critical acclaim and rave reviews, and in late 2023, *Celebrity Ascent*, her sister, came into service. We are back. We are stronger. The lesson I learned? While a pandemic or something else might knock you down, with resilience, no one can count you out.

8

The Boomerang

"Give out what you most want to come back."

**Robin Sharma, Canadian writer
and leadership expert**

We all have innate superpowers that help us get to where we want to go. We work hard to develop them and reflect on what they are as we gain new experiences and embark on new areas of business or our careers. Your superpower could be one particular skill or a combination of your strengths, knowledge, inherent qualities, and experiences that make you unique. We all use our superpowers in different ways. We all grow and develop things that we become good at—and I've described in the previous seven chapters what

I have worked hard at over time and believe my superpower is. And all the experiences and lessons I have learned along the way have helped me strengthen and hone it.

So, What Is *My* Superpower?

What do I believe is the one thing that defines my leadership style? The one thing that I accentuate to be the best leader I can be?

To help guide me to a conclusion, I decided it would be helpful to look up the definition of "superpower" as I contemplated my own. Here's what I found: "*Your most positive and powerful personality asset that influences, persuades, and inspires others to follow.*" As I read this definition, I thought, "Is that possible?" To have just one personality asset that can do all that? I'd always thought my superpower was the sum of my parts. I'd considered it the combination and culmination of all the traits I've previously described—firing on all cylinders, as they say. I thought of my superpower as the combination of all of that alongside my innate desire to create change and make waves. I thought the combination of drive, nurturing, trust, integrity, instinct, courage, optimism, risk-taking, and vulnerability was my superpower. Apparently not. Because the definition of a superpower is the *one thing* that is your most positive and powerful personality asset that influences, persuades, and inspires others to follow.

And then it hit me.

Never Let Each Other Down

As I have thought about evolving as a leader over time, and as I have become a more experienced and mature leader myself, I've learned that leadership, just like life, is a boomerang. You get what you give.

I've always believed this. As we all internalize and assess who we are, what we do, and what we want our advantages to be, we bring all of these to the forefront of how we lead every minute of every day, in every interaction we have. And that comes back tenfold. Just like a boomerang.

> "I've learned that leadership, just like life, is a boomerang. You get what you give."

Over time, I have tried to become better at this, and it's not easy. But by trying to be better, you will naturally lead yourself and your teams forward, and this will help you build your brand and your business. As a result, you will accomplish great things.

This idea of the boomerang of leadership relates back to the discretionary effort that people give you—not because it's their job but because they really care, as I mentioned in chapter four. And this is because they know *you* really care. I have so many examples of how the boomerang method of leadership creates a unique environment built on mutual investment in each other's success and caring. I would like to share a few of them.

One day, I was in a leadership meeting. It was a small group, just five of us, and our discussion centered around an off-site leadership meeting the others had just had. During the discussion, one of these leaders said that she found herself getting too involved in certain parts of her areas of responsibility that she shouldn't have to. I asked her why she did that: Was it because that was her nature and a leadership opportunity, or did she not think her team was capable? She said, "I do it because I don't want to let you down." That was not the answer I expected. And it really hit me.

Thinking about it, our company's culture is created based on the principles, behaviors, and expectations I have of myself. One thing I never want to do is disappoint or let anyone down who is counting on me. But somehow, I hadn't realized that my desire and behaviors to ensure I didn't let anyone down were creating the same desires and behaviors within those I worked with every day.

Many people were interviewed for this book. Not by me; the woman who was helping me complete this book's proposal thought getting to know me and my style of leadership would be important for us to understand as we set about selecting the areas and lessons that might be the most valuable and impactful to the readers—that is, all of you.

As I was writing *Making Waves*, I had the opportunity to read many sound bites from those interviews. I thought this chapter would be a good place to include some of them. As I have done throughout the book, I have removed names to protect the innocent! If they are reading this, though, I hope they recognize themselves, and I want to thank them from the bottom of my heart.

> *"At the end of the day, Lisa wants to have fun. She has high expectations, and she delivers on them. She genuinely cares about the brand [and] the people, and that means a lot. I want the brand to do well because I want her to do well. She has a strategic mind and a nurturing and caring soul. Her people and her brand are always top of mind."*

> *"Lisa is real. She's genuine, and she cares. No matter how hard my job is some days, I know she cares about her team. She's appreciative. And yet we all know we've got to succeed. Celebrity is more entrepreneurial, creative, and inventive. We try things that are sometimes uncomfortable. There's something special about this brand."*

Part of me wishes that people weren't worried about disappointing me or letting me down. But then I realize that's part of our secret sauce—our superpower. My superpower. I am grateful that the culture we have created together is one of an unwavering and mutual desire of wanting all of us to succeed.

I don't want to be Pollyannaish about never disappointing or letting each other down. I want to be clear that despite all of the positive and powerful examples of the culture we have created where none of us want to disappoint each other, I have in fact been disappointed quite a few times.

Though many will tell you they don't want to let you down, it's going to happen anyway. And probably often. People will tell you they believe in the culture you have established and the integrity by which they are all committed to abide, but later you may realize that this isn't the case. When this has happened to me, it has significantly affected me. Every time. Like a punch in the gut. My profound disappointment in those who have let me down takes me a while to recover from. I take it personally.

But that's another lesson I hope you learn from me: Don't do that. I've realized that I am working with human beings. Imperfect human beings. You can't take things personally. I shake disappointment off after a while, and I don't let it lessen my belief that the vast majority of the people I work with every day are not going to let me down. But I am still pragmatic that it will happen on occasion.

Despite the occasions that do happen, I choose to stay committed to my unwavering belief in the boomerang style of leadership and its contribution to a leader's superpower: when, as a leader, you have enabled, developed, and led your people in such a way that they do their best whether you are there or not. Like when we were the first ship to come back into service on June 26, 2021, and I couldn't be there. That was an incredible moment, another one where I experienced the true power of the boomerang.

The boomerang is also symbolized in our Edge Series of ships, which has been so special to Celebrity for so many reasons. It set the brand on a totally different trajectory when it was first introduced and continues to do so as we introduce the rest of the series into the brand and the marketplace.

"She is a woman leader who stands out. She is customer-centric, and she has never avoided challenges. The fact that it was a challenge never scared her. She is always collaborative, pursuing top talent and people who are willing to leave their ego at the door. She really raised the bar around fresh insight, newness. She has the vision but also a high-level trust in her close-in team. She's always had tremendous heart and integrity."

Every time I look at Edge, I'm reminded of the boomerang. The dozens of people involved in this project who went "all in" to make it a huge success. I remember being so grateful during the process of designing the series. Grateful to so many. Without their support and belief in what we were doing, we never would have ended up where we are now. If I keep throwing the boomerang out, the reward of it coming back is priceless.

Show 'Em You Care

As I mentioned earlier, it's critically important to keep evolving. While consistency in leadership is important, so is evolving your leadership style—either over time or in certain situations or circumstances. I've evolved, building different muscles for different reasons during different times. Early in my career as a sales and marketing leader, I wasn't as empathetic.

At that time, it was only about driving, hitting the numbers, achieving targets. I felt I needed to suppress some of the more nurturing and caring qualities I have because I thought they would make me appear weak.

When I moved into operations, engaging with our crew made me tap into my innate nurturing and caregiving qualities because I wanted to make sure our crew members were treated well and because I am a person who genuinely cares about people. I always have—from the time I was a young girl taking care of my sisters to the time I grabbed my first-grade classmate's hand and walked into the classroom with her so she wouldn't be so afraid and would stop crying. Leaning into my caring leadership style eventually became a key component of my superpower. And it started when I came into operations in 2005. Up until that time, I hadn't understood how that innate characteristic was so important to my success and to the people I worked with every day—not until I came into a position of leadership where I was leading a crew.

"Leaning into my caring leadership style eventually became a key component of my superpower."

So much changed for me in how I led as soon as that happened, as soon as I got to meet all of the crew and realized I was a key figurehead to them, someone they looked to for inspiration and their own ability to be successful, someone who was also a critically important advocate. I knew how much they'd given up by leaving their families, friends, and loved ones for months at a time to work on our ships. I witnessed their unwavering desire to please and do a great job. They do and give so much, and they deserve to be treasured. They deserve my commitment to them. They've earned it. In operations, I soon realized that I had to evolve myself to evolve the culture. I did that by just allowing myself to be me. It is my natural tendency to care for and to take care of people. And it works.

I don't know why caring was not a trait I'd practiced as much before my start in operations. Maybe the areas I previously worked in didn't need as much caring, or maybe as I became a more experienced and more mature leader, I realized a caring style was a strength, not a weakness. Like other women leaders, I believed that caring might make me appear weak. But I realized it was time to change that. And for the many years I have been involved in any part of the operations of our brands, I have made it a priority to show 'em I care.

I often wonder if our crew really understands how much I care about them, even though I have made many cultural, structural, and operational changes to show them that I do. I have also worked extremely hard to create an environment of inspiration and motivation. But I still wonder. We have so many ships, and they are spread all over the world. Can our crew truly understand what they mean to me? And then situations occur where I am reminded that, yes, in fact, they do know how much I care.

A very special moment for me happened on the day we took delivery of *Celebrity Beyond*. I was with the new president and CEO of the company and my new boss. We were in the Grand Plaza right after the ceremony, and all the crew were gathered for our celebration. It was the first time I was able to address the entire crew of the ship. When I was introduced, the crew was so very gracious in their reaction. After we were back in the office, about a month or so later, he and I were talking about delivery day, and I will never forget what he said to me: "The crew loves you. It's palpable. You can feel it." He's perceptive and intuitive, so I knew he really meant it, and that meant so much to me.

Another time, I was on the ship and running to a meeting in one of our suites. The woman crew member helping me get to where we needed to go told me that she was very happy to see me back on board again. And then, out of the blue, she said, "I hope you know how much we all love you." Wow. That just blew my mind. I was a little taken aback and didn't even know how to respond. All I could think to say was, "You've got it backward. I hope you know how much I love all of you. You all are out here working so hard every single day, doing such a great job for our guests, each other, and Celebrity. You are the heart and soul of our brand."

And as I read through the comments from crew members who were interviewed as part of the process of writing this book, I am touched yet again.

"Lisa is humble and approachable. The moment I met her, I literally fell in love with her ability to encourage people, her care for crew members, her awareness of what's going on. She is an amazing leader."

"What differentiates Lisa as a leader from the rest of the pack is her human side. She doesn't suffer from a personality crisis at all . . . she knows who she is. She makes us feel like we're all a part of the family. She is the mother figure."

What I've learned from all of these interactions and quotes is that, yes, people will know when you care. Even if you are on the other side of the world. As leaders, our actions speak louder than our words. What is most rewarding for me is when my crew feels the same way I do. The best part of all of this is that our crew doesn't just do what they do to make a living and bring money home for their families; they also do such a wonderful job because they know I genuinely care about them, so they, in turn, genuinely care about the ship and our guests—and me. Priceless. The boomerang.

We're All Equal

At the beginning of my time in operations, it was quite common and probably natural and understandable for the crew to be nervous and intimidated when leadership was coming onto the ships, whether it was to visit or sail. They didn't know what to expect. I remember thinking, "I need to change this."

It took some time to shift that way of thinking. But over time, it did change. I wanted our crew to know that while I was leading the brand, I was also their equal. I work for them. I appreciate everything they do. They are the reason Celebrity exists. It's their service and caring that keep our guests happy and coming back. Is everything perfect when I visit the ships? No. Is it my responsibility to evaluate what's happening and make recommendations and observations to ensure our standards are always met and that we are always improving? Yes. Do I do that? Yes. But it's how I do it that matters. As a leader, it is always important to come from a place of respect and gratitude, both in good situations and in situations that require feedback for improvement. I never give feedback that would make a crew member feel bad. I never want the leaders or crew on board to worry about a visit from me. By evolving our approach and style, when the other leaders and I come aboard the ship, people are excited to see us and disappointed if we don't visit or sail with them as often as we can. This is a very big win. A captain from our fleet said:

> "As a leader, it is always important to come from a place of respect and gratitude, both in good situations and in situations that require feedback for improvement."

Lisa is different. She's very approachable, very driven. She motivates people with just her presence. She's very authentic, and that gives you a sense of trust. She's goal oriented, and she shares her vision.

I was also quite flattered by an article that was written during the *Beyond* launch in November of 2022. Christopher Muther from the *Boston Globe* wrote:

When she walked around the ship during the naming ceremony cruise, passengers wanted to talk to her and take selfies with her. People didn't step out of her way because she's the big boss. They were drawn to her.

Of all of the lovely things he wrote about me, *Celebrity Beyond*, and Celebrity, that really touched me.

And that's a superpower. **People will do a great job when they know you care about them. And when they do, they will care about you as well.** While many will say that it's natural for people to have a healthy fear of their bosses, I never want that to be the primary driver of how I motivate people to do well.

I've also learned through all of the stories I am relating that, at the end of the day, people work for people. Yes, the pandemic caused people to reevaluate their careers—that's a given. But when it comes right down to it, the real reason people stay in workplaces or stay engaged is because of the people they work for. I've learned that I want and need to be the leader people *want* to work for. They have too many other options. As a leader, we get what we give. That's the magic of a strong and healthy culture. That's the priceless power of the boomerang.

The X Factor

The gift from the universe (and from my parents) is being a woman. I consider being a woman a definite superpower. In more ways than one. I use the disproportionate amount of attention that I get due to that fact to shine a light on Celebrity and build our brand.

I remember when I was appointed to this role. My phone did not stop ringing. I was like a unicorn—a rare sighting in the type of role I was in at the time. Each time I took one of those many calls or had one of those many conversations, I was asked: How does it feel to be a woman CEO? How does it feel to be the first woman CEO in your company? How does it feel to be the first woman in your company to join the C-suite?

The more I was asked those questions, the more irritated I got. I was overwhelmed by that reaction to my appointment. I hadn't expected it. I'd never thought about the fact that I was a woman. I just worked hard, did a great job, got great results, and finally got the position I deserved. But everyone else wanted to make a big deal of it. And then I had an epiphany. I decided to "go with it." I learned to use it as my superpower.

My opportunity to have a louder voice and get invited to a lot of places that would help my business and help others. So off I went.

Being a woman is a superpower in the vacation business. Did you know that 80 percent of a family's vacation decisions are made by women? Eighty percent! That's a lot.

As a woman in this role, I'm asked to attend and speak at many events where there are a lot of influential people. Many of them are professional women executives. They take vacations. They decide where their families are going to go. They care about the same luxurious experiences Celebrity delivers as part of our guest experience. These women support women-owned or women-run businesses. A match made in heaven. Our brand is perfect for these women and their families. I have garnered a lot of interest, press, and business for Celebrity with that as my superpower.

I also use this opportunity to help others (which, by the way, also helps the brand). I believe much is expected from those to whom much has been given, and I also believe that "there but for the grace of God go I." **I've learned that, as a leader, it is our responsibility and obligation to give back.**

I do a lot of philanthropic work so that I can give back and offer a lending hand, voice, and support to those who need it. By being involved in this philanthropic work, I network with many other professionals in our community—both men and women. Being in those circles benefits our community at large and our business. These business leaders become advocates and supporters of Celebrity and even book their vacations on our ships.

I use my superpower as a woman to bring others along with me. I feel like sometimes I am the poster child for gender equality. Maybe that's to be expected. And, sure, I have made it a point to help advance women in an industry that is woefully short of them. However, I have brought just as many, if not more, men along with me. More on that in the next chapter. But for now, I'll just say this: I've learned that becoming the CEO of Celebrity or any other company or brand should mean nothing to any of us if we are not reaching back and lifting others up with us.

> "I've learned that becoming the CEO of Celebrity or any other company or brand should mean nothing to any of us if we are not reaching back and lifting others up with us."

It is well documented and understood that women leaders have unique traits that create business success. That is more validation that the X factor is a big component of my superpower. Empathy, humility, persuasiveness, entrepreneurial spirit, and resilience are more prevalent in women, and as you have read about my journey and my lessons learned along the way, it is clear that they are skills that are always at the forefront of how I lead. And these skills that are due to my X factor help build my boomerang superpower of getting back what I put out there in the universe.

The End Game

One of the ways I guide myself in anything meaningful that I am undertaking is by starting with the end in mind. It's akin to writing the press release that I spoke about in chapter six. What do we want it to be? What is our end game? What are we trying to accomplish? That can be any number of things. It's important to know what your end game is so that you can chart your course to get there. For me, it was to put Celebrity on a differentiated trajectory that resulted in a stronger and more well-defined brand generating significantly better performance—and to create a unique culture while doing so. There were many things that I realized were important to achieve that. And I set upon a methodical way to get there. And I knew that without a strong and unique culture, none of it would be possible. Our culture is what brought our ships back into service and our crew back to work. The number of guests that book their next cruise while sailing with us on their current cruise is a testament to how much our guests love our experience, our crew, and our brand.

Again, it all goes back to the boomerang. Circular leadership. The higher the stakes, the bigger the job, the more important the boomerang becomes. My style of boomerang leadership that I have dialed up isn't the only way to achieve these results, but it certainly is one way that works for me, my team, and Celebrity. Being a leader who happens to be a woman, I have focused on my combination of attributes—nurturing, courageous, bold, risk-taking, innovative, values-based, creative, driving, ambitious, and empathetic—to lead over twenty thousand people toward achieving a common goal while feeling empowered, appreciated, cared for, and engaged. This superpower has pushed us all to achieve things we never thought we could. This superpower has created a boomerang that comes back to me every day. And it's the reason I will keep throwing good things out into the universe and wait for them to come back to me.

Pay It Forward

"For the great achiever it's all about me; for the great leader it's all about them."

Alan Mulally, former CEO, Boeing and Ford

As leaders, I believe it is our duty and responsibility to advocate, empower, and to give people the opportunity to shine. **I have learned that whatever we accomplish is not accomplished alone, and it means nothing if we can't or don't bring others along with us.** It is our obligation and responsibility to support others to achieve their dreams, to give them credit for what they contribute, and to give them the opportunity to chart their own successful course. I've also learned that when you shine the light, the reflection of that light shines back on you. Nothing I've wanted to accomplish was going to happen for me without the support, creativity, passion, effort, and intelligence of the village of people and professionals I have worked with along the way.

Paying it forward and shining the light so others can accomplish their dreams is the first thing I think about when people ask me how it feels to have attained what I have in my career. To me, it's not so much about what I've achieved; rather, it's the excitement in the opportunity to bring along others on this journey. I have the influence to lift others up and to help them accomplish their dreams and aspirations.

Diamonds in the Rough

For me, it's about paying it forward and shining the light, whether it's the entire organization coming back from the pandemic and being the first to set sail from a US port or helping an individual, a "diamond in the rough," do something they've always wanted to do but didn't think they were capable of, had the support for, or would have the opportunity to achieve.

I see these diamonds in the rough around me all the time. They are brilliant at what they are doing, but not everyone sees it. So, I ask myself: How can I help them grow? How can I be an advocate for them? Whether they are young and just beginning or have been doing a great job for years and just need a breakthrough moment, I know I can help them accomplish more.

This has been a great outcome of the evolution of our corporate culture. It is important to me to lift others up so they believe they have opportunities that they never might have thought possible. As our brand was growing, I wanted them to know there was so much opportunity. Or, as Captain Kate always says, "If you can see it, you can be it."

Thank Me by Doing the Same for Someone Else

Quite a few years ago, one of those diamonds that I uncovered, who had worked for us for over twenty years on the ships, came into my office. He'd started in an entry-level position in our dining rooms, had worked his way up into management positions on board, and was now in a management position shore-side. Never in his wildest dreams did he ever think this current position was going to be an option for him.

"Do you have a minute?" he asked.

"Sure," I said. "For you, anytime."

"I just wanted to tell you that I don't know how I will ever be able to thank you for making my dreams come true." He had tears in his eyes.

I remember telling him, "You don't have to thank me. You deserve everything you have achieved. But here's what I'm going to ask you to do. You need to do the same thing for other people—you need to pay it forward and help others make all of their dreams come true."

And he promised me he would. And he has.

While it's everyone's responsibility to pay it forward, it starts with me. I model this every day because it's who I am and because I want other leaders in our company and on our ships to do the same. They have accomplished so much, but they need to pay it forward. The reflections of the lights are so much brighter when we are shining the light on others. We are all illuminated when that happens.

I remember talking to another gentleman whom I had the amazing good fortune to meet and hire for a position we were looking to fill over a decade ago. He had just come off some difficult circumstances in his professional life and was looking for a new and different start. I knew he was special, as did all the others who interviewed him. He needed this new opportunity, and we needed his stellar talent. So we hired him and gave him the chance he needed and was looking for. And he has done an incredible job for our company. He is unbelievably talented, creative, and intelligent, and he has continued to evolve our brand in an area that is extremely important to our success. He has since been promoted many times.

One day, I was in his office visiting him. I noticed a photo of a house on his wall, and I asked him about it. He told me the only reason he was able to buy that house for his family was because of the opportunity we gave him. He hangs it there as a reminder, and every time he looks at it, he feels gratitude.

That was a powerful moment for me. I had no idea the depth to which he was so grateful for the chance and continued opportunities he has had because of the amazing job he has been doing. When you pay it forward and give others a chance and the space to grow, when you empower them to do the best they can, they usually do.

And when they tell you something like that, it's incredibly rewarding—and continued motivation. Our ability and intention to pay it forward changes people's lives in ways we will probably never understand.

> **"Our ability and intention to pay it forward changes people's lives in ways we will probably never understand."**

Our Shining Star: Captain Kate McCue

I was humbled when I read this in the *Boston Globe* on December 8, 2022: "Lisa isn't a reason why I came to Celebrity," Captain McCue said. "Lisa is *the* reason why I came to Celebrity. She is the reason that I stay with Celebrity. I have been approached by other cruise lines, but Lisa's the one that put me in the captain's chair. Lisa's the one that keeps me in the captain's chair, and wherever she goes is wherever I will go."

I was overwhelmed by these powerful words. Thank you, Captain Kate. The immense admiration is circular.

Captain Kate is a rock star. Would she have become a captain if we'd never met? Absolutely. Probably not as quickly, though. Would anybody else have shone the light on her as much as we do? I don't think so. I'm proud that we've given Captain Kate the ability to accomplish her dreams and create a powerful platform for other women mariners and fans all over the world. The first American woman to ever captain a mega ship, the first woman captain for Celebrity, the first captain to sail a ship out of a US port post-pandemic, and the first woman to take a new ship out of the shipyard in France. Quite a résumé. Not to mention that our guests love her, our crew members love her, and over three million followers on social media love her.

Captain Kate always wanted to be the first woman to take a ship out of the shipyard. And she got that chance with *Celebrity Beyond* in 2022. It was a momentous occasion for all of us, Captain Kate, our teams, and the brand. We knew it would get a lot of attention and focus. And it did. And we were all so thrilled for her.

During the pre-inaugural sailings for this magnificent new ship, all our guests wanted to talk to and take a photo or selfie with Captain Kate. They were lined up every time she made an appearance. She was a magnet. Usually during these events, it's the president and CEO of the brand that gets this type of attention. But not this time. I didn't even come close! And that was just fine with me. She deserved it. I wanted this to be her time, and I was so happy that this was happening for her. I watched her bask in the attention of it all and relished those moments for her.

Finally, on the last night as the events were coming to an end, my husband and I were going to retire for the evening, and we bumped into Captain Kate's husband, who had joined us for the celebration. We made it a point to say goodbye to him on our way to the elevator to our room. He gave me a big hug, and when we moved away from each other, his eyes were filled with tears. "Thank you," he said. And then he looked over his shoulder to his left. I turned, and there was Kate in all her glory, surrounded by people who were just in awe of her. She had all of the light on her, and she was loving it. Having great fun with our guests. I remember thinking how much it meant to her husband, what a special moment that was for him, and how proud he was of her.

Brothers Ascend at Sea

Another beautiful "pay it forward" and "shine the light" story is of our captains of *Celebrity Ascent*. For the first time in our history and in the history of the industry, we named two brothers as co-captains of this brand-new ship. An honor in and of itself to be the takeout captain of a new ship, it's twice the honor when you are able to name two captains who happen to be brothers. Eleven years apart in age, the brothers have now both worked with Celebrity for more than two decades.

They spent their careers growing from entry-level positions on the bridge to achieving captain. The older brother, Captain Dimitris Kafetzis, was the youngest-ever captain to reach this position at Celebrity until his younger brother, Tasos, broke that record. Dimitris was Tasos's inspiration and role model their entire lives and the reason why Tasos decided to be a captain. They have been shining examples of the new generation of caring captains who are mentors to others on their bridges and who have shown genuine caring and appreciation for our crew.

It has been my joy to work alongside them for more than fifteen years. When we were deciding on who should captain our newest ship, *Celebrity Ascent*, I wanted us to once again make history, pay it forward, and shine the light on these amazing brothers, so we named them as co-captains.

I knew this would be an honor for them and that they would be excited, and they were. What I didn't know, and could have never anticipated, was how much it would impact them emotionally. It was a dream come true for them. Something they never thought they would ever be able to do. They had always hoped they might be able to sail together, but they'd never dreamed they would be the two captains to take out one of our new ships for the very first time. They have repeatedly told me they don't know how they can ever thank me for giving them this opportunity. Their bond is one of the strongest I have ever seen. And we have made their dreams come true.

Of course, our marketing and social media team did an amazing job announcing them, and they have become an overnight sensation, going viral on social media with over thirteen million views as of this writing. We all remember conducting the interviews so we could create the terrific video for their announcement. It took longer than we thought because of how emotional they both were as they were telling their story about growing up, their incredible bond, and their ultimate journeys to captain. The video is beautiful. They are new celebrities. And I couldn't be happier for them.

I never get tired of making people's dreams come true. It is so tremendously rewarding as a leader and one of the most selfless things we can do.

The Reflection of the Light You Shine

A big deal was made about my being the first woman to cut steel in the shipyard where we build all our Edge Series of ships. At this ceremonial event and very important milestone in shipbuilding, I remember looking out at the audience and the many women who were there.

One of them was the head of PR for the shipyard. She'd been in the role for many years and has recently retired. She said, "Thank you for being the first woman to do this. It's important for all of us." I

"I learned in that moment that having the spotlight shine on me for being the first creates a reflection that shines right back on others."

learned in that moment that having the spotlight shine on me for being the first creates a reflection that shines right back on others. These other women felt like they were participating and being noticed and recognized in a way that they hadn't been before. And they were. Because they could see it, they realized that they could be it.

I feel such an immense sense of joy from this, but I also feel a big responsibility. That is why I have been intentional about enabling other women to experience things that they didn't know or think were possible. Another reason why I continue to pay it forward and shine the light back whenever I can.

A Chance Encounter

Many years ago, I had the opportunity to speak to a group of Mandela Fellows who were part of a leadership series of African students and professionals who, through their academic achievement and contributions toward giving back and helping Africa, were selected to participate in this program. I was asked to come and speak to the group about leadership. It was an honor, and as I read their résumés, I was so impressed with their contributions to their countries and the fields they had chosen for their professions.

At the end of my comments, I took questions from the audience, and a young woman who had her hand raised stood up to tell me that she had been looking forward for me to come and speak to them because she wanted to tell me her story and ask for my help. And that she did. For about three minutes, she told me all about her educational background and her experience to date in her country. She was a graduate of the Regional

Maritime University in Ghana, had her MBA, had experience working on cargo ships, and her dream was to work on the bridge of a cruise ship. But she had not been able to make that dream come true.

As she had asked for help on the ships she was working on, she was repeatedly told that her dream was never going to come true. She was told to go home, get married, and have children because no cruise company was going to hire her. She was also told that women mariners are bad luck on ships. She told me I was her last hope. And she asked me if I could please help her.

I had tears in my eyes by the end of her story. I thanked her for having the courage to ask for my help and promised to do what I could. The others stood up and erupted in applause. At the end of the session, I got her contact information. Then I did what any good leader does: I delegated this to our head of Marine and asked him to check out her qualifications and, if all looked good, to please find a way to hire her.

Easier said than done. We soon discovered that the Ghana Maritime Academy was not recognized by the International Maritime Organization or our flag state of Malta, so we could not hire her. *Yet.* For an entire year, our head of Marine worked with both organizations and finally got the academy approved by both.

Needless to say, it was a very proud day when I received a photo of five young women of color kneeling in front of the sign for the Ghana Maritime Academy holding the Celebrity flag. Thirteen months later, I welcomed onto one of our bridges the young woman who'd had the courage to ask me for help. She was the first woman of color we hired on our bridges, but not the last. We have hired many more cadets from the Ghana Maritime Academy throughout the past few years.

> "I learned that as leaders we have the opportunity and influence to change our industries for the good and to help drive equality in many ways."

Equally important, I learned that as leaders we have the opportunity and influence to change our industries for the good and to help drive equality in many ways. We changed the industry and the trajectory for all students who graduate from the Ghana Maritime Academy. We singlehandedly worked with the International Maritime Organization to create opportunity for these graduates to work in the broader maritime industry. Opportunities to pay it forward are all around us. They aren't always easy, but they are so rewarding when we are able to make them happen.

Be an Enabler, Not an Obstacle

As an outcome of my career path and of having so many different positions throughout the company and brands, I realize from personal experience that everyone is on their own journey. I also realize that sometimes we don't even know what path or journey we might end up taking, and that there can always be a fork in the road that you never expected.

When I was moved into that marketing position from sales that I told you about earlier, I vividly remember feeling that my career was derailed—when, in fact, it began a new journey and trajectory that I never expected. To this day, when I talk to the person who was my boss at the time about that situation, he reminds me of my initial reaction. He always asks, "Remember how I moved you into marketing and how upset you were?" Of course, I have to respond in the affirmative because it's true. Then he follows it with, "And how did that work out for you?" And we both laugh.

What that experience taught me is that I need to do the same for others. I need to create opportunities that will ultimately help people follow their own dreams and achieve things they otherwise might not be able to. I try to create a safe haven where people can experiment and try different things. The worst that can happen is it doesn't work out. To me, failure is lack of trying, and I never want to hold people back from what they want to accomplish. Even if they don't know it at the time.

It's important to identify opportunities for valuable and talented team members so they can grow and accomplish greater things. I recommend people for other opportunities that I am aware of so they can grow. These are hard decisions because oftentimes that means these great people might not work for us anymore, and it's difficult as a leader to let those people go. But it's the right thing to do. Many years ago, when I was vice president of operations at Celebrity, I hired a director of onboard revenue. She was a key member of my team for ten years. Smart, creative, transformational, and financially savvy, she was a big factor in the success we had for many years. And I made sure she was a key member of my team even as I was changing roles throughout a decade.

Then, one day I got a call from someone who was looking for a key leader on his team who would ultimately take over as president of the company. He described all of the attributes he was looking for. I immediately knew that this woman who was a key member of my team was the perfect fit. He did, too, before he even called me. But he wanted me to be the one to say it so that it came from me that she should take the position.

So I called her into my office to discuss the opportunity. I also told her I thought she was perfect for it and that she should take it. It was hard for both of us, but she did. And she has done extraordinarily well and has ascended into the higher role faster than any of us thought she would. That's our job as leaders—to develop and help people grow and discover their best selves by recommending and encouraging them to take opportunities, even if it means moving into a different area of the company or even another company all together. It was tough for me and for Celebrity, but it was the best thing for her. I paid it forward. Someone did that for me, and I needed to do it for her, too. I could have stood in her way. I could have said, "Absolutely not!" when I got the call. But that would have been the wrong thing to do. I couldn't do that after all she had done for me, Celebrity, and our company.

Happily Ever After

With all I've been able to do for Celebrity in my time as president and CEO, my best memories are "happily ever after" stories. Life at sea can be difficult for families. You are separated for months at a time, and if you are a parent and away so much of the time, it can become a burden for your family. And even though people get married and start families knowing what the situation will be, the actual lived reality sometimes causes people to rethink what they signed up for.

Such was the case for the wonderful man and his family in my first "happily ever after" story. Several years ago, this gentleman was a key member of our shipboard leadership team and knew nothing other than a life at sea. At the time, he had a wonderful wife and a new baby daughter. A truly lovely and happy family. They'd met on board, gotten married, and started a family. But at a certain point, his wife decided that it was too difficult having him at sea and not with them. And he could not think of a life away from the sea. Neither of them wanted to separate, but they didn't see a way forward under the circumstances.

It was such a sad dilemma. They loved each other, and neither of them wanted their marriage to end, but he couldn't live off ships, and she couldn't be with someone who lived on ships.

They separated. Knowing how heartbroken they both were, I kept thinking about how I might be able to help.

So, I got a bit creative and asked him to come to Miami for a short-term project that was getting underway. We needed help, a shipboard leader was the perfect choice to lead it, and I knew that he would be fine with a short-term project on land as long as he would be able to get back to sea afterward. So he came and led the project, and it ended up taking a bit longer than we anticipated. He enjoyed it, though, and was eventually able to bring his wife and daughter to Miami. Even though they were separated at the time, he was able to see his baby girl for long stretches.

As he became more used to this shoreside gig, I asked him if he would be interested in a shoreside position that had just come open. I knew if I could get him to agree to this position, there might be a chance that his marriage would work out and the family would be reunited.

He thought about it, and he decided to take it. He told his wife about the Miami-based position, and she was very supportive. He convinced her to come to Miami often and to stay for long periods of time, and, once again, he was able to see their little girl for extended periods of time, too. Slowly but surely, they rebuilt their connection and got back together, and for many years they have been thriving and living happily ever after in Miami.

Sometimes you can pay back in a way that makes a profound difference in people's lives when you have the ability to do so. The marriages and children that I have been a part of helping and uniting are numerous. I'd like to share about just one more.

I get flowers every year from a gentleman whom I helped reunite with his girlfriend many years ago. They had been assigned to different ships, and he had asked if I could get them assigned to the same ship again. I made a call. It happened. They are now off ships and married with three children. I get flowers each year on his first son's birthday. The card reads, "It's my son's birthday, and if it weren't for you, he wouldn't be here. Nor would I have this beautiful family."

People's personal happiness is just as important to me as their professional careers. I learned long ago that if you can help someone achieve a balance of personal and professional happiness, you, as a leader, will as well.

Another true reward of leadership: all the "happily ever afters."

The Real Reward of Leadership

I have chosen to share just a few meaningful stories here. There are many, many more. The reason I share these "pay it forward" stories is because this is the part of being a leader that is the most rewarding, makes me so genuinely happy, and is the part that I love the most.

Of course, I also love our great results. And I strive every day to make them even better. I am still on that journey with the twenty thousand people I work alongside daily. I love the green traffic lights I see as we track against our KPIs—and I really *don't* like the yellow and red ones that I sometimes see. All of this is critically important to my personal success as well as Celebrity's.

But, at the end of the day, my only success is because of our people at Celebrity and the people in our company who contribute to our success. It's because of them and because I've enabled, encouraged, and tried to inspire them to do their best. They are living their dreams. They are happy in their lives. They're using their creativity and passion, and my job is to ensure they get the credit and recognition they deserve.

When a crew member or one of my teams tells me how much they love working together and how much they love what they get to do every day, when their lives change for the better and they get to realize their personal and professional dreams, and when I have the ability to contribute to any of these things in any way, that's the ultimate reward of leadership. And that's how you are ultimately able to make waves.

10

Full Steam Ahead

> "Success is no accident. It is hard work, persever-
> ance, learning, studying, sacrifice and most of all,
> love of what you are doing or learning to do."

Pelé, one of the greatest soccer players of all time

Aptly titled, this last chapter of *Making Waves* is focused on the first full year of our comeback, our forward trajectory, and the continuation of my amazing journey. Coming back hasn't been easy. In fact, it's been harder than we thought it would be.

The COVID-19 pandemic—with its short-term, massive impact on the industry, the business, and our brand—weighed heavily on our ability to stay focused on our long-term future.

But, patience, perspective, and staying the course to build on the strength of the Celebrity brand to bring us back to where we left off before our pause in business—that's what's gotten us through. Through the many worrisome times, we have maintained our focus on the future of our brand, and that has pushed us through the starts and stops to make it to the other side.

Today, everyone is once again focused on the long game. They are focused on the future, and nothing is going to stop them. As we proceed full steam ahead, we only look back at the past few years to celebrate our resiliency and to remember that while we may have been knocked down, we persevered, and today we are sailing toward our bright and positive future.

Beyond Our Wildest Dreams ... Almost

In April 2022, six months later than originally intended, we delivered *Celebrity Beyond*. Even with all the starts and stops caused by the shipyard shutting down and the availability of contractors and subcontractors to finish the work, there was never any question we were going to build and take delivery of the ship. It was just a question of when, because of the one thing we couldn't control: the pandemic.

Beyond's delay meant her first season would start in Europe. Our beautiful flagship would make her debut in Southampton, United Kingdom.

I clearly remember the pre-inaugurals for so many reasons. The response we got from our team and when we finally introduced her was heartwarming and wonderful. While we certainly weren't out of the pandemic, things were becoming more normal, and cruising was coming back in a big way. We were filled with excitement to deliver this ship, which was beyond our wildest dreams and anything we'd ever imagined, and our guests, too, were filled with excitement to be celebrating such a beautiful ship and introduction. There hadn't been much to celebrate over the past couple of years, and everyone was more than ready.

Just prior to the introduction, we were full of anticipation. There was so much to look forward to. We were anxious to see the reaction of people when they saw the changes we'd made from the first two ships in the series. *Beyond* was so different from *Edge* and *Apex* that, in many ways, it was like a completely new ship. The changes were meaningful and spectacular. The Grand Plaza, Rooftop Garden, and Sunset Bar, with its multi-level terracing designed by Nate Berkus and beautiful Mediterranean feel, were a few of the more transformational changes.

We were excited to show her off to the press and our travel partners. We arrived in Southampton a few days early to put on the finishing touches and then welcomed everyone aboard. It was the who's who of press from Britain, Europe, Australia, and key national travel press from the United States. Everyone loves the Edge Series, so they were so excited to see what was new and different on *Beyond*. They were excited to see Captain Kate, who, as you know, was the first woman ever to take a ship out of the yard and the first woman to ever start up a brand-new ship. The combination of wonderful things happening were very special for us and generated a lot of excitement. It was a very wonderful time, and we enjoyed every moment of it, despite the challenges we were still facing.

Stops and Starts

While the delivery and launch of *Beyond* could not have gone better and validated that we were coming out of the pandemic and going full steam ahead, the months prior had been tough.

It was disheartening for me and the team that despite all our hard work, despite getting our ships back into service, and despite our beautiful new *Celebrity Beyond*, 2022 was still a tougher year than we were anticipating. We were all disappointed. We're driven, we're competitive, and we want to win, but staying motivated and engaged was tough. As a leader, I learned to celebrate all the small wins so the team would get through the year and focus ahead to 2023. And we did get through it, but it wasn't easy.

Building Momentum Even in Headwinds

Believe it or not, of all the years of the pandemic, 2022 was the toughest for me. My expectation was that we would be in a better place than where we ended up. By midyear, all our ships were back in service. A monumental task and a huge accomplishment, and cause for celebration. We had waited so long for that day. And it was finally here. But while we were continuing to build momentum throughout the year, we were not seeing the usual "rewards" we were working so hard to achieve. We wanted to be celebrating collectively across every area of our brand and our business. We deserved it.

The headwinds were monumental and continuous. But we stayed the course and navigated through all of them together. We rallied and did whatever we needed to do—together. It took everything we had. And, as the leader, I learned that I needed to keep encouraging everyone to help them through the myriad of issues and headwinds that we were facing every day. And I had to convince everyone that everything was going to be okay. And, by the way, they were doing the same for me.

Validate, Validate, Validate

Now back to building, we were also back to creating a five-year strategic plan. We looked at macro trends as part of our corporate strategic plan and how those trends related to Celebrity and our guests. We also contemplated if our strategy against these trends might look different in the post-pandemic world we were now operating in. We had all been through so much these past few years, we had to validate that we were looking at everything through the correct lens.

For Celebrity, it was very encouraging for us that we learned we were still firmly in the bull's-eye of what our guests want from their vacations with us, the things that were important to them, and why they chose us. And we also learned that other consumers who resemble our guests also want the same things in their vacations. They want to experience new places and cultures around the world, they want to eat excellent food, and they want to be in an environment that creates a sense of well-being. These things had always been our focus and the key pillars of our brand. And now that we were coming out of the pandemic, we were finding that these things were even more important than ever. This made us confident in our future, especially given that there are sixty-three million consumers we identified who fit our demographic and psychographic target in our primary markets.

The benefit of going through the strategic planning process in 2022 was that we once again had validation that Celebrity was focusing on the things that mattered to consumers who cared about the same things we do. This was just like the evaluation we undertook in 2020 to validate our direction and brand positioning to ensure our comeback was going to be stronger than our setback. A lesson I've learned throughout my years of brand building is that it's important to continue to revalidate your brand proposition to ensure you are meeting the demands and desires of the consumers you are going after. You need to know that your brand identity is strong and grounded in ongoing meaningful insight and research and data. Had we been off course, our comeback would have been significantly jeopardized.

We realized that while our world might have stopped for a while, the things our guests and target audience cared about had not changed. Quite the opposite; those priorities had only grown stronger. Our optimism in the future was renewed because we found out that people wanted to live their lives and explore the world again. Having to take a time-out from experiencing the world was as tough for them as it was for us.

This was an important outcome for all of us at Celebrity. Me. My team. Our entire shoreside employee base and our teams on board. It restored the confidence that was being challenged during a very difficult comeback year. As a leader, I learned once again that patience, courage, resilience, and optimism needed to stay at the forefront of how I was leading. Even on the difficult days. Some days I was better at that than other days. I am far from a perfect leader and still a work in progress. An important lesson for all leaders.

> "I am far from a perfect leader and still a work in progress. An important lesson for all leaders."

Off-the-Charts Engagement

One of the things that is great about our company is that we are very focused on employee engagement. We take it seriously and continually monitor how our employees—ship and shore—are feeling about working in our company, how they feel about their leaders, and how engaged they are as employees. Of all the companies, across all industries, that conduct these types of surveys, we have among the highest scores. We are proud of our corporate culture, and our results prove time and time again that we have a highly engaged workforce. That said, even with the tough year Celebrity had in 2022, with the starts and stops of coming fully back into service and the ramping up of our demand and business, we still had the highest employee-engagement scores in our company. I'm very proud of that.

This is a testament to our leaders and their leadership. I don't take credit for it. I do take credit for surrounding myself with a team of leaders who in turn surround themselves with leaders who, even during the most challenging of times, create an environment that is caring and engaging. Our collective leadership team keeps everyone focused on our outcomes, the brand we have built, the positive and forward momentum we are experiencing, and the innovation and creativity that keeps us strong and a force to be reckoned with, even as we sail through rough waters. I've learned that difficult times are those that prove how strong your leaders and your culture really are.

> **"I've learned that difficult times are those that prove how strong your leaders and your culture really are."**

And that's why, even though we were not the brand achieving all of its performance goals, we had the highest engagement scores. How people feel about working at Celebrity is incredible. It's not just the crews on board; it's our shoreside teams, too. Like the people at our call centers who were managing customer expectations and frustrations as we dealt with all the protocols, restrictions, and regulation changes. Like our PR team that oversees our guest communications and was responsible for updating protocols constantly—practically minute by minute—when countries kept changing them.

But we got through it, and as the year progressed, it got better and better each day. And toward the end of the year, we even had historic booking days during the key weeks when so many people book their vacations for the following year. That continued to build our optimism and confidence for a strong 2023. We were full steam ahead, with full ships at the end of the year and over the holidays.

As we turned to the next year, the percentage of business we were building, over and above 2019, was incredible. We continually built significantly more business than ever before. Our travel partners were pretty much back to where they had been before the pandemic. All that energy we'd used to keep ourselves going throughout the last few years was now surging toward the future—full steam ahead. You could feel the weight lifting off people's shoulders as that momentum continued, and there was a new pep in everyone's step as our business got better and better.

Weebles Wobble but They Don't Fall Down

As I think back on it, the business we were generating during our busiest booking time in early 2023 was a stellar testament to the strength of our brand, the strength of our messaging, and the strength of our team. And it's also a testament to the strength of our travel partners, who were back and continuing to support us as they always had.

This momentum resulted in the best customer demand that we had ever had. It was giving us tremendous forward momentum. Our teams were energized and motivated, and we were putting the finishing touches on *Edge V*, which will be the next great ship for Celebrity, making her debut in late 2025, and the last in our transformational Edge Series. And we were starting to think about the next series of ships for the brand. Wow. My, had things changed for the better.

Have you ever heard, "Weebles wobble, but they don't fall down"? That was our industry, and that was Celebrity. We kept getting disproportionally punched, but we didn't stay down. We bounced right back up. We kept going. Today, our brand is strong and business is very good. Our guests are happy. We were back to full steam ahead.

The Tin Man, the Scarecrow, and the Lion

As I worked on this book and outlined my leadership journey and the many lessons I've learned along the way, I started thinking about the things that rise to the top of importance as a leader. There are so many. And as I was thinking about an analogy that would be helpful, I thought about the Wizard of Oz and the friends Dorothy made on her journey to meet him.

I thought about the scarecrow and why he wanted to go and meet the wizard. He wanted a brain. As a leader, I've learned it's certainly important to be smart. You need intelligence and experience to succeed. No question. We've covered that a lot in the previous chapters.

Then I thought about the tin man. He wanted to meet the wizard because he wanted a heart. Leading with heart and leading out loud with it garners loyalty and employ-

> **"Leading with heart and leading out loud with it garners loyalty and employees who are invested in your success."**

ees who are invested in your success. We achieve everything through others, and caring leadership allows us to experience the boomerang—getting back what you give.

And, last but not least, I thought about the lion. And that brought me to the epiphany that, above all else, **leaders need to have courage**. It's been quite a journey, leading Celebrity through our engineered turnaround with the Edge Series of ships and through the global shutdown of the past few years. It took courage to get through the comeback and the unexpected struggles that came with it. Never underestimate the power and importance of courage.

Courage has led me through my entire career. It led me through the early part of it when I took a chance and embarked on a new career in an industry I knew nothing about. It then took courage for me to accept a position that took me away from where I grew up to begin a new journey—not having any idea where it would lead to. When I asked the team to change the pricing for *Celebrity Edge*, it took courage to hold firm even though my team wasn't completely on board with my decision. When my sister was losing her courageous battle with cancer in the next room, it took all the courage I had to show up for my team, to get through the day and a launch that was critically important for all of us.

It takes courage to keep going in the face of adversity, to stay the course and to face the doubts and fears of yourself and others. It takes courage to face head-on the questions and concerns that will constantly come your way. To be a leader at all takes courage. We aren't in it for the short game; we are in it for the long haul, navigating an ever-changing environment in our rapidly changing world. It's easy to give up.

But every morning, I got up, got dressed, and lived to fight another day. Throughout my career, I've done what I've believed I had to do at the time. I've done things differently and charted a course that has been some parts my choosing and other parts not, always looking ahead with positivity at what was on the horizon. I've tried to be a leader who doesn't blindly follow others and who tries to keep thinking differently so that our brand would continue to be a leader and leave others in our wake. That takes courage. Walking into a boardroom when you know things aren't rosy, going against your team at times to follow your instinct and create a new category of cruising, changing things that have always been done a certain way—all of these things take courage.

I've tried to be courageous above all else. Like *Fearless Girl*, the bronze sculpture in Manhattan's Financial District. I know that I've made a few waves and more than a few mistakes along the way. I believe the waves I've made, whether transformation and innovation in ship design or focusing on gender equality in an industry that needed more gender balance, have changed Celebrity and the cruise industry for the better and for the long term. My hope is that these changes will have a lasting impact long after I'm done.

My motivation for everything I do is to make a difference. Making a difference takes intelligence and heart—and so often takes courage because when you make waves, you sometimes have to turn the tide. I've learned that you have to stand by your values, stand by your teams, stand by your brand, stand by your decisions, and stand by your instincts to create a lasting legacy. I am still working on creating mine. But just like the scarecrow, the tin man, and the lion, I've learned that it's within all of us to do whatever we want to do. None of us need the Wizard of Oz. He is just a man behind a curtain.

The Next Chapter

I've learned another lesson during this incredible and long career and as a leader: It takes a tremendous amount of courage to decide when it's the right time to reassess what you want to do with the time you have left. That decision is never easy for so many reasons, but at some point you have to make it. For me, I put off embarking on my next chapter or stepping away for a few years. I have had a myriad of reasons or excuses: "I'm not ready." "I can't step away until we are fully back." "How can I leave my team and brand?" "How can I leave my crew?" "I'm still too young to step away!" (I'm really not.) Oh, yes, I talked myself into continuing time and time again, even though I knew I needed to get to the ultimate decision that I should be making. And that probably happens to many of us who are at this stage of our lives and careers. But I finally had the courage and decided that time had come for me. **Oftentimes, we can't separate who we are from what we do because they become so intertwined with time.** When you still have passion and energy for what you are doing, the decision becomes more and more difficult. For many who are reading *Making Waves*, you may be just beginning to think about your career or

> **"It takes a tremendous amount of courage to decide when it's the right time to reassess what you want to do with the time you have left."**

just starting on your journey, so this particular section might not resonate—yet. Someday, it will.

It takes even more courage to step away from a career and an industry that you have been a part of and has been a part of you for almost forty years. We can keep talking ourselves out of leaving by convincing ourselves that the timing isn't right—saying to ourselves, like I've said to myself, "I'll just keep going for a little while longer." It takes courage not to do that and to just close your eyes and take the leap. There will always be a next chapter. You really do owe it to yourself to stop. Get off the merry-go-round. Turn it over to someone else. There is so much left to do elsewhere that can and will be different but might be just as great. There is so much more out there to fulfill us. There is so much more to give back. We are all multidimensional. Our careers and our lives should reflect that. You can't do other things if you are fully consumed by one thing.

It's been a beautiful ride, an amazing career that I never dreamed of, in a fabulous company. It's been a ton of hard work, more than a few sleepless nights, a few tears, and looking back, I'm grateful for every single moment of the journey. I wouldn't change a thing. And looking ahead, I can't wait to continue making more waves. I'm not done yet. On to the next chapter. Full steam ahead.

ACKNOWLEDGMENTS

There are so many people to thank for all they contributed to *Making Waves* and my career. I am going to do my best to capture them and want to admit right up front that I am going to forget someone or something. Although unintentional, I hope that, if you are reading this book and recognize any situation we were in together, you accept my sincere and heartfelt thanks for contributing to this amazing journey and career of mine.

I would like to thank Jan Miller and the Dupree Miller team. My literary agent who believed in me and my story from the very beginning and stuck with me through the many years it took to bring *Making Waves* to life. You have been an advocate, a mentor, a friend, and someone I admire greatly.

Matt Holt and the BenBella team for taking a chance on an unknown woman and author by publishing *Making Waves*. From our first conversation, I knew that BenBella was the perfect publisher for me, and I will be forever grateful to you for reading my proposal and wanting to publish my leadership book.

Sarah McArthur, thank you for writing this book with me, and for helping me find my voice and tell my story. Your guidance, experience, patience, and insight made *Making Waves* so much better than even I thought it could be. The fact that you were so invested in wanting to help me share my story and my lessons was the ultimate compliment.

Susan Lomax and Jill Spencer, thank you for helping guide me through the process and being my sounding board for how *Making Waves* came together. Though I was a reluctant book author, you both kept inspiring and encouraging me that this book had to be written and were with me every step of the way. And beyond that, you are two of the greatest and smartest women I have had the pleasure of working with. Thank you for caring about me, and I hope you know how much I care about the both of you.

Adora English, Katherine Hill, Wes Smith, and Carolyn Spencer Brown, thank you for getting me started and getting my book to the proposal stage. A lot of iterations and stops and starts, but without all of you, we never would have gotten there.

All of my company colleagues throughout my almost forty-year career, thank you for helping me achieve all I have and for sharing in my successes and challenges. Your partnership and support are the reason that *Making Waves* is possible.

All of my Celebrity colleagues and leadership teams (ship and shore) who stood beside me and lifted me up as much as I hope I've lifted all of you up. What a ride. Many of you are still on it, and I can never express the gratitude I have for all of you. I will continue rooting for you as you take Celebrity and our company to the next level. It has been an honor and a privilege. You have my respect, admiration, and affection—and always will.

The Celebrity crew: Where do I begin? It has been the biggest honor of my life to have worked with you to deliver the best guest experience for the best brand in the world. You have inspired me for decades. Being your colleague and witnessing your passion, commitment, professionalism, and loyalty were the highlights of my career. I love you all and am so grateful to all of you.

Captain Kate McCue, you didn't have to, but the fact that you said yes forever changed me and Celebrity. Watching what you have done to change the face of this industry has been a joy. You are a rock star. I know your light will continue to shine brightly. I will forever remember, and be grateful for, the day we met and I entered your universe.

My coaches and mentors throughout the years, especially Claudy Jules and Jane Stevenson. You have made such a meaningful and important difference in my life and career. I will never be able to thank you enough.

Our travel partners who have supported me for almost four decades from that fateful day in May of 1985 when I knocked on your doors asking for your support and all the years after. You have contributed to my success and career in so many ways, and I am so grateful to all of you.

Bob Sullivan, thank you for the beautiful foreword. I was so touched and overwhelmed by your words. I have so much respect and admiration for you and all you have done in and for our industry. Knowing you for over three decades, I cannot tell you how much your integrity and insight into the entire travel industry impresses me and how much we all count on you to tell the truth and to continue to shine the light on this amazing and important industry we are all in.

To all who took the time to write a testimonial for *Making Waves*, thank you so very much. You have made my career all the more special for knowing you, collaborating with you, and being able to call you not only colleagues but also friends. I have always said that one of the greatest joys of my career was meeting incredible people along the way.

Thank you to my bosses throughout the years who believed in me, sometimes even more than I believed in myself.

Michael Applebaum, we started together, and you supported, encouraged, and promoted me for thirteen years. Thank you, my friend. While I have not been able to call you my boss for many years now, I am truly grateful for everything and even more grateful I am still able to call you my friend.

Dan Hanrahan, you were right. Forcing me to move when I kicked and fussed and didn't want to worked out very well for me, indeed. The major moves and accomplishments that were the impetus for this incredible journey were all because of you. Thank you for being the first to believe in me more than I believed in myself.

Richard Fain, your wisdom, guidance, mentorship, support, belief in me, and finally saying "yes" and giving me my dream job changed my life forever. While you always told me not to thank you because I deserved what I achieved, I told you that while that may be true, "Thank you" is still something that I will always say to you anyway.

Jason Liberty, my colleague and friend for so many years and my boss for just a couple, thank you for supporting Celebrity and me and Godspeed as you take the company to new and great heights. I will continue to cheer you on.

And now for the people who mean everything to me. My family.

Mom and Dad, thank you for bringing me into this world and helping me become the person I am today. You have shaped me in so many ways—many that you realize and many that you don't. Your unwavering love continues to propel me forward.

My nieces, to whom this book is dedicated, and my nephew Brody—our prince. I am so proud of all of you and love you all so very much. I hope that you have been and will always be proud of Auntie. You have been at the top of the list of those whom I have never wanted to let down. Now go and make a difference in the world that I know you will and that the world needs. Thank you for being my inspiration and compass.

My brother-in-law, Anthony Meloro, thank you for being an amazing father to my nieces and nephew, the brother I never had, and an unbelievably wonderful husband to my baby sister, and for all you have done for our family and me.

My son, Benjamin, his wife Joanne, and their children Jocelyn, Jake, and Greyson, my biggest supporters and cheerleaders. You have given me so much love and made my life so much richer because I had the wonderfully good fortune of meeting your dad. You all make me proud every day, and I love being in your lives.

My nephew Sayer, you are the most wonderful man, and your mother was always so proud of you—just like I am. Thank you for your goodness and love. My first nephew and godson, I am forever grateful at how much closer we have become over the past few years. I know your mama is watching over all of us.

My sister Dawn. Gone too soon. We were supposed to grow old together. You are still with me every day in so many ways. I still have that "strongest woman alive" mug you bought me. You told me you bought it for me because you didn't know anyone who was stronger than me. But the truth is that you were the strong one. And I admired and loved you so very much.

My sister Bobbi. I love you more than anything. Thank you for being my sister, friend, daughter, and advisor—even though you tell me over and over again I am a terrible client. My life was forever changed for the better the day you were born. Thank you for so generously sharing your children with me. They have been the lights of my life. I love you to the moon and back, and I have always wanted to make you proud and would do *anything* for you. But you know that. And so does my husband. ☺

Andre, for over forty years you have been by my side. Through good times and bad. Through the lean years and the not-so-lean years. You never made me feel bad or guilty when this crazy career consumed me. You supported me even when you were worried that my mantra of never giving up might mean

I would get hurt or disappointed. You supported my career and have never resented or been threatened by it. You have cheered me on. And you have loved me through it all, even when the badass CEO in me came out. Thank you for everything and the life we have made. I love you.

And to the readers of *Making Waves*, thank you. Thank you for being interested enough in my journey and all I have learned as I navigated a career that was unique and unexpected. My true motivation was to tell my story through the lessons I learned along the way to make the navigation of your careers and lives easier. If I have helped in any way—big or small—that will be my true reward.

ABOUT THE AUTHOR

Credit: Martin Castaneda

Lisa Lutoff-Perlo (LLP) is Vice Chairman of External Affairs for the Royal Caribbean Group, one of the leading cruise companies in the world with three award winning brands: Royal Caribbean International, Celebrity Cruises, and SilverSea Cruises. She previously served as President & CEO of Celebrity Cruises from 2014 to 2023, the first woman to take the helm of a Royal Caribbean Group brand, and one of the few women in the world at the time leading a multibillion-dollar brand. Lisa shares her extraordinary and inspiring four-decade journey along with her successes and failures, highs and lows, and the meaningful lessons she learned along the way using her unique combination of smarts, heart, and courage, which enabled her to break the glass ceiling and leave behind a lasting legacy.

Lisa began her career with Celebrity in 1985 as District Sales Manager and trailblazed her way to the top over the first thirty years of her tenure. Along the way, she ultimately transformed and redefined the relaxed luxury cruise experience with the launch of the bold and innovative Edge Series of ships in 2018. Immediately hailed as game changing for the industry and included in *TIME* magazine's "World's Greatest Places" list, the ships have driven unprecedented demand and propelled the brand's financial performance.

Throughout her tenure as CEO, she demonstrated exceptional vision, strategic acumen, and an unwavering commitment to excellence. Her leadership not only propelled her organization to new heights but also served as a shining example for professionals across industries.

A purpose-driven leader, she catalyzed cultural progress in the two-hundred-year-old cruise industry by appointing the first American woman to the position of captain and the first West African woman to work on the bridge of a cruise ship; making history with the first all-female bridge and leadership team sailing in 2020; and, ultimately, increasing Celebrity's percentage of women on the bridge to 32 percent, far exceeding the industry average of 2 percent.

Lisa's expertise extends far beyond the boardroom. She has developed a profound understanding of the dynamics of leadership, effective communication, team-building, and the pursuit of excellence. Her unique blend of practical insights and personal anecdotes creates a captivating narrative that resonates with audiences of all backgrounds.

Whether it be addressing a room full of executives, entrepreneurs, or aspiring professionals, she has the remarkable ability to connect with individuals on a personal level. Through her engaging storytelling and compelling delivery, she has fostered an environment of inspiration, igniting a desire for growth and transformation within each listener.

Armed with invaluable insights gained from years at the helm of a thriving enterprise, she shares her wisdom and expertise with a wider audience. Through executive coaching and high-profile keynote speaking, she continues to inspire, motivate, and empower individuals and organizations, helping them unlock their true potential and achieve unparalleled success.

She has won numerous innovation, inclusion, and lifetime achievement awards for her groundbreaking efforts to chart a new course for the cruise industry and actively lends her expertise to numerous international and regional organizations and boards.